I0358078

Blissful

Devotions

A Mother and Daughter's Journey of Faith
90-Day Devotional

ALMA J. CHAMBLISS AND ARLEATHIA D. CHAMBLISS WRIGHT

Blissful Devotions: *A Mother and Daughter's Journey of Faith, 90-Day Devotional*

1st edition 2023

Published by ACES Publishing Group.

Book Cover and Interior Design by ACES Publishing Group

Dedications

To my beloved children, Harold, Cynthia, Wanda, and Arleathia, and with love and cherished memories of Daphany, I dedicate this book to you. I dedicate this book of spiritual devotions to you because it is a dream I have had since I was 16. These devotions are a testament to who God is and continues to be for this family. As I began to build my relationship with Him, I prayed and asked God for a husband and children so that I could love them the way God loves me. When he gave you to me, I knew my life would be about love. I began to raise you with the love of God and to love one another. I have always and continue to pray that he always watches over you and that no harm will come to you. I also pray that I live to see you grow in happiness and love with your own families. You are the best children. I am so proud of who you have become. I owe it all to God and could not have done it without Him. For this, I am so thankful. I hope this book fills your heart with much love and admiration for Jesus. Please cherish my testimonies and use them for your own relationship with him. Seek Him first and trust Him. I love you always.

~ Momma

Dedication to my mom, Ms. Alma J. Chambliss

"This book is dedicated to my incredible mother, my collaborator, my rock, my sunshine, and my greatest inspiration. I hold you in high honor and deep adoration. You have been the epitome of a loving mother, a shining example that others aspire to have. Your unwavering love has never faltered, even during moments when I may have mistakenly believed otherwise in my younger years. You have imparted invaluable wisdom and knowledge to me. Now that I am older, I comprehend why you have always been there for me, standing by my side. It is because of your boundless love that you have worked, worshiped, and protected me. When I shared my idea of writing a devotional with you, my heart overflowed with joy as you revealed the collection of devotions you had written over the years. I have always sensed a profound connection between us, and that connection is rooted in our shared love for God. Thank you for believing in me through every circumstance God has guided me through. Your unwavering support means the world to me."

To my son, Mr. Dameion Dismuke

"I dedicate this book to my son, Dameion, with heartfelt pride and love. From the beginning, I was taught the importance of keeping God as the priority in life. With that belief in mind, we joined Beulah Missionary Baptist Church and enrolled you in faith-based Christian Academies, ensuring you received a solid foundation in Christ. I cherish the memories of reading devotionals to you before bed when you were little, knowing that it provided spiritual protection when I couldn't be there. My deepest prayer is that you continue to build a personal relationship with the Lord, and that He watches over you every night. I am immensely proud of the man you have become, in the name of Jesus. This book is dedicated to you, as a symbol of my love and faith."

Preface

After reading several books by friends and family, my daughter, Arleathia, came to me with an exciting idea. She was inspired to write a daily spiritual devotional about her experiences growing up and her relationship with God. As her mother, I was thrilled to see my daughter so filled with the spirit. So, I took Arleathia to a place where I kept my devotionals that I had been journaling for years.

Arleathia was amazed by after seeing my devotionals and saw an opportunity for us to collaborate and share our testimony with the world. Together, we wrote, edited, and compiled our devotionals into Blissful Devotionals, a collaboration between a mother and daughter that demonstrates our love for God, our family, and each other.

Table Of Contents

Day One

Pray About All Things

Philippians 4:6-7 New International Version (NIV)

Do not be anxious about anything, but in every situation, by prayer and petition, with thanksgiving, present your requests to God. 7 And the peace of God, which transcends all understanding, will guard your hearts and your minds in Christ Jesus.

The Bible tells us that we should not worry about anything instead pray about everything. Thank Him for all He has done. Pray for him to supply your needs. If we do this, we will experience God's peace which is more wonderful than man will ever understand. His peace will guard our hearts and minds as we live in Christ Jesus.

I know this because I have been worried and afraid. When a storm came through town and caused damage to my house, believe me, I was nervous and worried. This situation caused me to experience anxiety. Instead of trusting God and being obedient to His word and not worrying about anything, I became sick with anxiety. When my husband and mother became ill, I did not know what to do. All I remembered is to turn to him in prayer asking for strength through their sickness. Once I made my request known, He gave me peace of mind. The Holy Spirit brought me to this scripture John 14:27 and Philippians 4:6-7. It helped me to believe that His word is true. Once I began to believe His word, I began to have peace and there was no more worrying.

We should think and meditate on these things that are true, honest, just, pure, lovely, and whatsoever things are of good report. Think about things that are excellent and worthy of praise. For example, you may have been unemployed for some time and found it hard to find employment. With much prayer and thanksgiving, and God blessed you with the job you have always wanted with the right income. It also could have been a time even though you were not working, praise be to God, he supplied all your needs.

We should be encouraged to replace our anxieties with love and grateful prayers. The peace of mind comes from our inner being where we trust God to answer our prayers. It is a blessing when we go to God in prayer anytime or any place. He is waiting to talk with you. Praise the Lord.

Let us Pray:

Father God, who sits high and looks low, we come to you not only praying for a few things, but for all things. Help us to refrain from being selective in our prayers for your word tells us to be anxious about nothing, but in everything by prayer and supplication, with thanksgiving, let our request be known to you. In Jesus name. Amen

Song to Ponder: *Pray – CeCe Winans*

--Alma Jean Chambliss

Day One

Describe a time you were anxious about some things, and as you prayed, you realized that His promise is true.

Day Two

My First Prayer

Read: Matthew 6:9 New International Version (NIV)

"'Our Father in heaven,
hallowed be your name,
10 your kingdom come,
your will be done,
on earth as it is in heaven.
11 Give us today our daily bread.

The verses of scripture in this prayer are the first verses I was taught by my mom growing up as a small child, which was also recited each Sunday morning in Sunday School. Every night before bed, my mom and I would get on our knees to say this prayer aloud. Between my mom and church, this prayer has been deeply rooted inside my heart and soul. My mind is programmed to automatically recite it as I hear it. Was this your first prayer as a small child as well? Did you and your parent(s) pray together before bed? Was this prayer recited out loud at your church each Sunday?

Jesus wrote this prayer. He taught His disciples how to pray along with crowds during His Sermon on the Mount. When I was a small child, my mom taught me how to pray as Jesus did, using the same scripture verses. As you read Matthew 6: 9-13, you will discover that Jesus taught His disciples how to pray and what to pray for.

Why is this prayer so powerful?

I believe this prayer is so powerful because of how Jesus instructs us to approach God. Jesus said that we should address God as 'Our Father' while honoring Him at the same time as 'Holy' having a nurturing and loving father/child relationship with Him. From His kingdom, we should ask God to grant us the desires of our hearts only if it is His will and not ours. Then, we should ask God to provide His word and the things we need from day to day such as our physical, mental, and spiritual wellbeing, which is our daily bread. We should also request for forgiveness for our wrongdoings such as our sins and forgive those who have wronged us. Therefore, confess to Him our wrongdoings and believe that God has the power to pardon those offenses, and free us from the bitterness and hurt that others have caused us. We all have weaknesses that we must pray for God to convict us when we are enticed to do wrong, asking Him to intervene on our behalf removing us from the situation. After these requests are done, praise the Lord, giving thanks for all He has already done for us.

Let us pray:

Our father which art in heaven, hallowed be thy name. Thank you for providing this prayer and teaching us how to pray. Thank you that as we learn this prayer, we will pass it on to others. In Jesus holy name we pray. Amen.

Song to Ponder: *Hymn - Hear Our Prayer, Oh Lord*

This is the air I Breathe – Byron Cage

--Arleathia Chambliss Wright

Day Two

How powerful is this prayer to you?

Day Three

The Crucifixion Of Jesus

Read: Matthew 27:31 New International Version (NIV)

31 After they had mocked him, they took off the robe and put his own clothes on him. Then they led him away to crucify him.

See how Jesus was mistreated before he went on the cross. People beat him and spit on him. They also made fun of him. Out of all the good he had done for them; they still did not believe in Him. I cannot believe how the priests went along with all that they did to Jesus. They were there with the crowd cheering the soldiers on. They told Jesus, if you are the Son of God, come down from the cross, and they would believe. Unfortunately, I am sure they would not have believed. Someone would have come up with excuses as to how Jesus came down from the cross.

Have you or someone you know ever been in a fight or insulted because of who they are, who or what they believe in by standing up for what is right in the sight of God? You may have done some good things for people who still mistreat you by insulting you and physically hurting you. Guess what; join the club. Remember the saying, if they did it to Jesus, they will do it to you. What is so sad, we as Christians are being crucified daily by this world of unbelievers. What makes it worse, Christians do things like this to each other all the while they are pretending to be Christ-like. Being Christ-like means, acting like Christ. Christ did not mistreat people.

We see every day how God takes care of us; how he protects us; how he heals us; and how he fed us, supplying all our needs, and we continue to not believe. Thankfully, He did not come down from the cross to save Himself. In order to fulfill the scriptures, He died to save us.

Let us Pray:

Dear God, we ask that you will please help our unbelief . Jesus gave His life willingly. He proved He is the Savior of the world by not coming down off the cross. When He died, He rose with all power in His hand. Thank you, Jesus, for dying for our sins.
In Jesus name, Amen

Song to Ponder: *He would not come down from the cross just to save Himself. –Keith Armstead*

--Alma Jean Chambliss

Day Three

Describe a time when you were being Christlike, and someone mistreated you.

Day Four

Encountering Afflictions

Read: ***Psalms 119:71 New International Version (NIV)***

71 It was good for me to be afflicted
so that I might learn your decrees.

What is affliction? Affliction is a state of pain, distress, grief, misery, sickness or sufferings and extreme hardships. Also defined as mental or bodily harm caused by self or other people. Have you ever encountered affliction? We have all experienced afflictions. People are jealous, mean-spirited, and manipulative. There may be someone jealous of your happiness. They may think that every time they see you, life looks good. When they never see you defeated, they can become jealous and mean. The people who are mean will hurt our feelings. Remember the saying, "hurt people, hurt people". If you're not careful, people will manipulate you into feeling sorry for them. You will do things you really do not want to do for or with them. These types of encounters cause affliction making you feel bad.

I remember being picked on in grade school, but God turned it around. That experience helped me to continue to be kind to others even when they are not kind to me. It also taught me how to choose my friends who had the light of the Lord. His light in others makes me happy. With the encouragement, love, and the spiritual teachings from my family, I realized as long as I had them and the Good Lord, I would be fine. Someone said, let your haters be your motivators. It was hard at times, but I made it through that affliction.

The scripture tells us that David was not only after God's own heart; he also kept his faith in God. Nevertheless, he was not exempt from affliction. In Psalms, David was writing about being afflicted by people. He was very popular in Israel. Regardless of his popularity, the people would still cause him pain and distress. These people were jealous, mean-spirited, and arrogant. They were heartless people, but David chose to follow God's law. He said in Psalms 119:69-70, 69 "The insolent smear me with lies, but with my whole heart I keep your precepts; 70 their heart is unfeeling like fat, but I delight in your law."

There is good news! Believe it or not, affliction is good for us. David said in Psalms 119:71, 71It is good for me that I was afflicted, that I might learn your statutes. Like David, even though our experience, being bullied, was painful, miserable, and damaging during affliction, Christ turns the outcome into good. When we may try to address the issue in our own way, we make it worse than it really is, causing extreme hardships. But, when GOD is in control, he shows up and shows out demonstrating His power over our afflictions.

God has access to every issue and provides the necessary steps we need to take to confront the afflictions. God gets excited about revealing His power to us. He is excited because this may be the time the affliction will draw you closer to Him. So, while we are drowning in our afflictions, we should learn His promises giving Him all the glory and the praise. Once we have overcome the affliction, our experience helps us create a personal testimony about how it was good for us as well.

Let us Pray:

Dear heavenly Father, thank you for letting us know that our afflictions were not made to harm us but for good. That they might help us learn your statues. Thank you that they are meant to draw us nearer to you.
In Jesus name, Amen.

Song to Ponder: *Draw Me Close to You – Marvin Winans*

--Arleathia Chambliss Wright

Day Four

Name some afflictions you have encountered and God stepped in.

Day Five

Loving Care And Kindness

1 Thessalonians 2:1-7 New International Version (NIV)

2 You know, brothers and sisters, that our visit to you was not without results. 2 We had previously suffered and been treated outrageously in Philippi, as you know, but with the help of our God we dared to tell you about his gospel in the face of strong opposition.

3 For the appeal we make does not spring from error or impure motives, nor are we trying to trick you.

4 On the contrary, we speak as those approved by God to be entrusted with the gospel. We are not trying to please people but God, who tests our hearts.

5 You know we never used flattery, nor did we put on a mask to cover up greed—God is our witness.

6 We were not looking for praise from people, not from you or anyone else, even though as apostles of Christ we could have asserted our authority.

7 Instead, we were like young children[a] among you.

Have you ever appealed to someone with loving care and kindness to convey the gospel of the Lord Jesus Christ?

Paul was up close and personal with his brothers and sisters about how much he cared for them with the kindness of his heart. He shared that he had no hidden motive speaking the gospel and was being obedient to the assignment that God gave him to share the gospel with other people. He was preaching the gospel that helps you through oppositions.

We should be like Paul speaking very gently when speaking about the goodness of God and all God has done for us. Have a caring heart for when you tell someone, 'God loves you'. Choose your words carefully allowing the Holy Spirit to tell you the words you need to convey the truth about the true and living God. You must not look to take credit for anything God has done. You should be obedient to His word. By doing this, people will see God in you and what you are doing is to please Him.

So, let us be encouraging and have tender mercies on our brothers and sisters in our Christian walk with our wonderful savior.

Let us Pray:

Lord, help us to be sensitive and caring as we serve others.
Help us to be loving and kind to others like Paul and as you are to us.
In Jesus name. Amen

Song to Ponder: *Goodness of God Cee Cee Winans*

--Alma Jean Chambliss

Day Five

Describe a time when you appealed to someone with loving care and kindness to convey the gospel of the Lord Jesus Christ as Paul did.

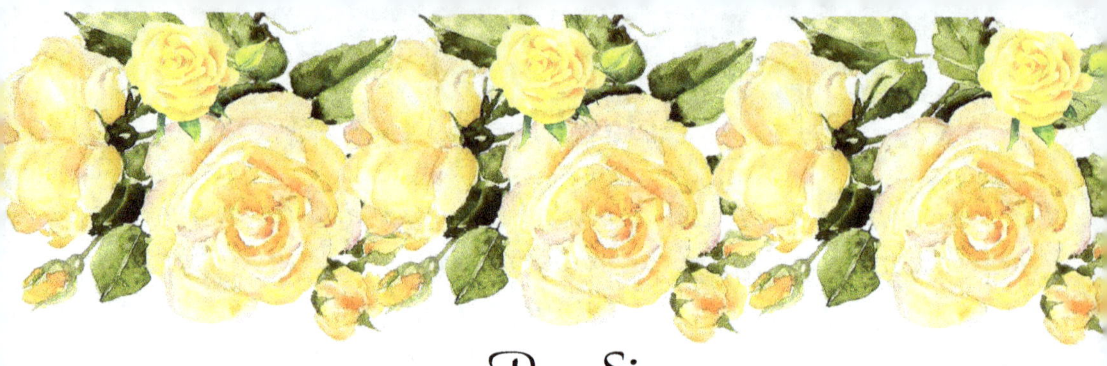

Day Six

In Times Like These

Read: ***Matt 14:19 New International Version (NIV)***

19 And he directed the people to sit down on the grass. Taking the five loaves and the two fish and looking up to heaven, he gave thanks and broke the loaves. Then he gave them to the disciples, and the disciples gave them to the people.

Remember when the government shutdown, the longest shutdown in US History? It was shut down in December 2018 for about 35 days, ending in January 2019. This decision left many federal workers wondering where their next meal and bill payments were going to come from. As a matter of fact, I received a text from one of those federal workers. They were asking for prayer and stating that their company informed everyone that they would be paid until the end of December, however, the next month was not promised.

Our people were suffering at the hands of the US government. Haven't we all depended on the government for as long as I can remember? Who should we be depending on? The answer is God. Ding, ding, ding! He said, "Lean and depend on Me". Glory to God! God used this time to be Glorified. I hope many believers saw the promise of God. He said in Deuteronomy 31:6, "Be strong and courageous. Do not fear or be in dread of them, for it is the Lord your God who goes with you. He will not leave you or forsake you." He goes on to say in verse 8, "It is the Lord who goes before you. He will be with you; he will not leave you or forsake you. Do not fear or be dismayed." Paul also promises in Philippians 4:19 "My God will supply every need of yours according to his riches in glory in Christ Jesus." Thank you, Lord.

There were churches who opened their doors to offer groceries, fed families a hot meal, and paid bills of those people who had been affected by the government shutdown. Glory to God. This should remind us of the story in Matthew 14:13-21 of how Jesus fed the multitude with two fish and five loaves of bread. After He looked toward heaven to bless the food, He gave the food to the disciples to feed the crowd. Praise be to God, Jesus was able to feed over five thousand men, women and children with only two fish and five loaves of bread. The point is, these churches demonstrated taking what they were blessed to have, then blessed everyone who asked for help.

Let us Pray:

Father God in heaven. Thank you for not leaving us and providing the things we need to survive the madness. Thanks for reminding us to lean and depend on you and to rely on your promises. God bless the churches in their act of kindness to feed the multitude. We ask these and other blessings in Your name. Amen

Song to Ponder: *Made A Way · Travis Greene*

--Arleathia Chambliss Wright

Day Six

Has there ever been a time like these where your needs were supplied where you were short on the rent or limited resources to meet your needs?

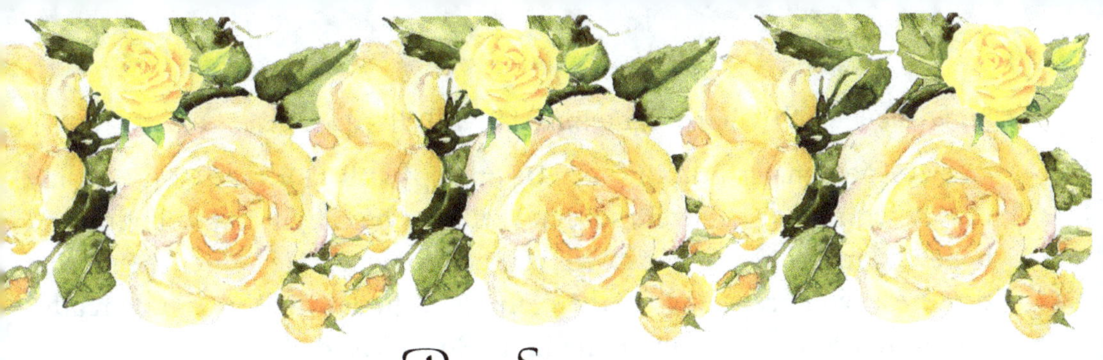

Day Seven

The Day Of The Lord Is Coming

2 Peter 3:10-13 New King James Version (NKJV)

But the day of the Lord will come as a thief in the night, in which the heavens will pass away with a great noise, and the elements will melt with fervent heat; both the earth and the works that are in it will be [d]burned up. 11 Therefore, since all these things will be dissolved, what manner of persons ought you to be in holy conduct and godliness, 12 looking for and hastening the coming of the day of God, because of which the heavens will be dissolved, being on fire, and the elements will melt with fervent heat? 13 Nevertheless we, according to His promise, look for new heavens and a new earth in which righteousness dwells.

Here, Peter is reminding us of what Paul said in his letters. We need to be careful of the naysayers who refuse to believe that Jesus is coming back. The Lord wants us to grow in the grace and knowledge of our Lord and Savior Jesus Christ. As a believer, let's focus on what the Lord wants us to do to prepare for His return. He wants us to remember the promise of His return while growing as Christians. He does not want us to perish but to repent of our sins.

When He comes back, He wants us to be ready. It is not going to be like in the days of Noah when the earth was destroyed by water. The next coming will be fire as described in Revelation. The bible says in 10-11 that the Day of the Lord will come like a thief in the night. It will not be good for those who do not believe in Him. Those who believe will not be surprised. We wait on His promise of a re-creation of a new heaven and a new earth where righteousness will dwell.

I am personally building a relationship with God and surrounding myself with other believers so that I will not be caught not knowing and believing in His word. What will you believe when He comes the second time? Are you preparing for the coming of the Lord? Will you be ready? We do not know the day or the hour. So, get ready.

Let us Pray:

Lord, help us to get our life in order. Please mold us into the person you want us to be. Help us to grow more every day in your word.
In Jesus name. Amen

Song to Ponder: *Everything's going to be alright, He's coming back. –Rev. Al Green*

--Alma Jean Chambliss

Day Seven

Describe how you are preparing for the coming of the Lord.

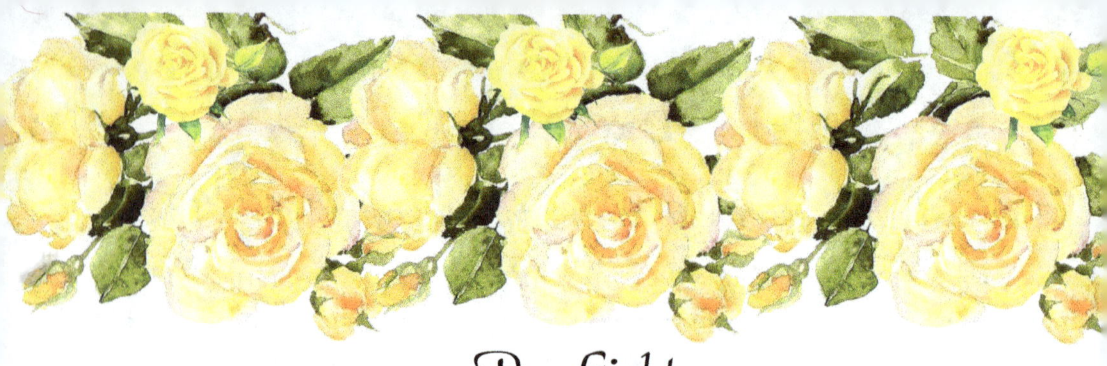

Day Eight

MEDALS vs CROWNS

1 Corinthians 9:25 New International Version (NIV)

25 Everyone who competes in the games goes into strict training. They do it to get a crown that will not last, but we do it to get a crown that will last forever.

I started running following my oldest sister, Cynthia Chambliss, and my brother-in-law, Clarence Daniel. We all participated in races in honor of my middle sister, Wanda Daniel, celebrating her survival of breast cancer and for breast cancer awareness. As a family, we started donating to many causes, signing up for races in the area and invited one another to participate if our schedule permitted. As a result of participating in these races, we were awarded participation medals for finishing the race.

The collaboration with other runners really made the races fun and motivating. My personal goal was to use the races to manage my weight, learn self-discipline and earn a medal for my efforts from each race. I set out to run a 5k each month for a race, then the next year, run a 10k each month. For every race, my motto is: I run for medals.

There could be two different races in life that give rewards. One race rewarding perishable medals that are given to winners who place. This medal does not last forever. However, the other race rewarding an imperishable crown made by God is given to servants of His race that lasts forever. Which would you prefer?

As an athlete in a physical race, seeking a medal in a race comes from the heart with hard work and self-discipline. It builds confidence during the race knowing what the outcome will bring for your efforts preparing for your reward. Considering all the training, running gear, the fellowship with other runners, the cause, the eating habits, and the early morning commitments, these are sacrifices to earn a perishable medal in the race.

As a Christian in a spiritual race, our efforts are to win the 'crown of glory' with the same intentions from the heart with hard work and self-discipline. Considering the same Christian sacrifices with a twist, we are trained to build a relationship with God by spending time with Him each day, wearing the Armor of Christ in this race, and praying for one another for encouragement. The only difference is that God is in control and will judge who gets the crown.

1 Corinthians 9:25 says "Everyone who competes in the games goes into strict training. They do it to get a crown that will not last, but we do it to get a crown that will last forever." Do not run any race aimlessly. Train to discipline your body and mind with self-control. Anything less, in your spiritual race, will disqualify you from reaching your ultimate goal, the Crown of Glory, the imperishable medal that will last forever.

Let us pray:

Father God, we come now to thank you in advance
for the crown of glory. The crown of glory that
You give that will last forever. We look forward to
seeing You at the finish line.
In Jesus name we pray, Amen.

Song to Ponder: *Run Until I Finish – Smokie Norful*

--Arleathia Chambliss Wright

Day Eight

Which would you prefer?
BUT God…

Day Nine

Jesus Gives His Power & Authority

Luke 9:1-6 New International Version (NIV)

9 When Jesus had called the Twelve together, he gave them
power and authority to drive out all demons and to cure
diseases, 2 and he sent them out to proclaim the kingdom
of God and to heal the sick. 3 He told them: "Take nothing
for the journey—no staff, no bag, no bread, no money, no
extra shirt. 4 Whatever house you enter, stay there until you
leave that town. 5 If people do not welcome you, leave their
town and shake the dust off your feet as a testimony against
them." 6 So they set out and went from village to village,
proclaiming the good news and healing people everywhere.

One day Jesus met with His disciples to give them specific instructions to go and cast out demons, heal the sick, and spread the good news proclaiming the kingdom of God. He told them specifically what to do. They were obedient by doing what was expected of them which would fulfill the purpose of God. On their journey, they experienced rebellion and hatred from the people. Jesus prepared them for this as well. He instructed them on how to deal with all types of adversities that they would encounter. Jesus gave them His power and authority for the journey ahead.

He told them not to carry anything with them. He did this to show them that they had to depend on him and his power and not their own provisions. He told them that when they visited, just stay long enough to deliver the message and keep moving. God would give them all they needed to accomplish His mission.

Has God ever taught you how to handle yourself while doing his work? I am sure He has given you specific instructions. He told me as I go spread the good news, do these things: (1) To seek Him first in everything. (2) I do not need anyone but Him. (3) Not to worry about tomorrow as it will worry about itself. (4) Be bold in the Lord. (5) The battle is not mine. It is His. (6) To ask, and it shall be given. (7) To knock, and the door will be opened. (7) He said He will never leave me nor forsake me. (8) To trust Him.

God will give us the same power and authority as he gave his disciples if we only ask. He has given us gifts to glorify Him. We must pray and ask for these gifts to be known to us and use them according to his will. Only Jesus can grant His power and authority. When you receive it, you must be obedient and use it to glorify Him. He gives us the instructions and commands in His word.

Let us Pray:

Lord, help us to encourage others and let them know that You have all power in your hand and with that same power we can do all things; Help us to trust You with their lives knowing that you can do anything but fail.
In Jesus name. Amen

Song to Ponder: *Power – Smokie Norful*

---Alma Jean Chambliss

Day Nine

Describe a time when you realize that you have the same Power & Authority as Jesus gave His disciples.

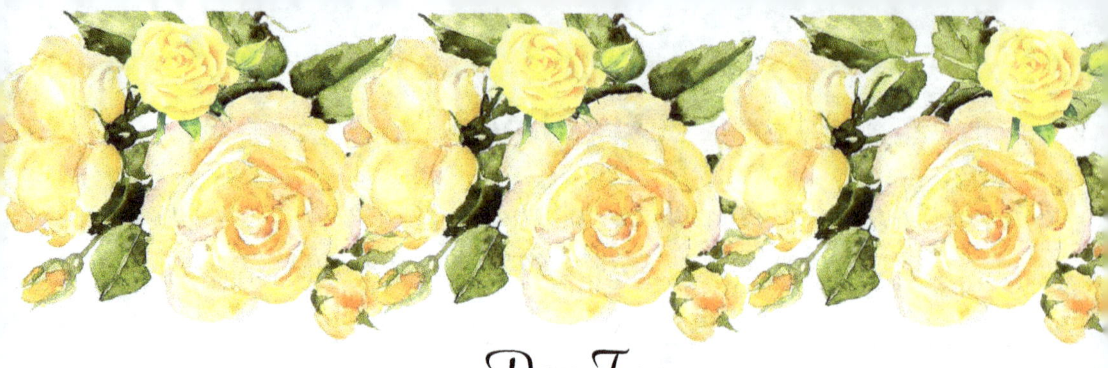

Day Ten

No Weapons!

Read: Isaiah 54:17 New International Version (NIV)

17 no weapon forged against you will prevail,
and you will refute every tongue that accuses you.
This is the heritage of the servants of the Lord,
and this is their vindication from me,"
declares the Lord.

This story is about Wanda, an African American Woman in her thirties. She was taking a shower one night before bed and while bathing, Wanda felt something unusual about one of her breasts. Trying not to panic, she yelled to her husband, Clarence, to come to the shower to examine her breast. They both agreed that something was different about the way the breast felt. So, first thing the next morning, Wanda called for an appointment with her doctor. The doctor examined her and sent her straight to radiology. A few days and a few tests later, the doctor diagnosed Wanda with Breast Cancer. Clarence and Wanda begin to experience a challenge of a lifetime.

African American Breast Cancer Alliance states that within the minority groups, 1 in 8 Women will be diagnosed with Breast Cancer in their lifetime and Breast Cancer is the 2nd leading cause of death. There are ways African American Women can prevent Breast Cancer through self-examinations, regular checkups, eating habits, wellness and exercise. Ladies, it is so important for us to know what breast cancer is, how it is affecting our communities, and ways to prevent it.

Wanda held her head high keeping her faith and adopted part of the scripture from Isaiah 54:17 – No Weapons! She knows that God promises that no disease from the enemy would kill her. She believed that she would succeed and survive the concern with breast cancer.

Wanda Daniel is my sister and has survived breast cancer because she took it seriously by paying attention to her body and caught it before it was too late. She is now a 25-year survivor. Living, loving and enjoying life with her family. Glory to God!

We all will have weapons that will form, but God promises that they will not prosper. Don't be afraid of the enemy and his plans. God is in Charge because He created the weapons. He has the say so if they prosper or not. God will do what he promised and stand by His word. He will be there to rescue you from the hands of the enemy.

Let us pray:

Dear heavenly father, thank you for not allowing the enemy to get to me. You taught me that weapons may form against me, but they will not prosper. You have stood on Your words to see me through. Thanks for fighting the battle for me. In Jesus name I pray. Amen

Songs to Ponder: No Weapons formed against me by Fred Hammond123 Victory – Kirk Franklin

--Arleathia Chambliss Wright

Day Ten

What weapons have formed against you that were ineffective because God said so?

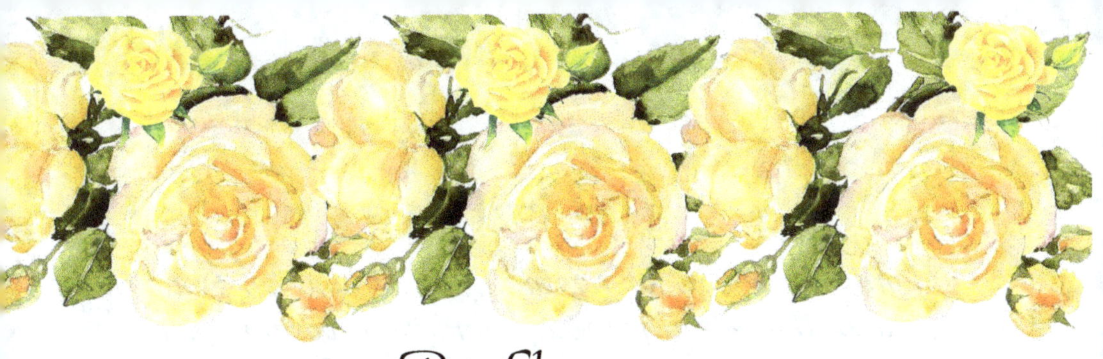

Day Eleven

God's Awesome Power

Psalm 72:12-20 New International Version (NIV)

For he will deliver the needy who cry out,
the afflicted who have no one to help.
13 He will take pity on the weak and the needy
and save the needy from death.
14 He will rescue them from oppression and violence,
for precious is their blood in his sight.

The psalmist speaks often of God's awesome power because God is in control of everything. Did you know that God has the power to do anything? He can heal the sick, raise the dead, prevent horrific events, at the same time provide all that you need. He is waiting for you to ask that His power rest upon you.

God's awesome power is in control of everything. Absolutely Everything! When you ask, let His will be done. He can help rescue you when you are going through domestic abuse or a stressful job. He can help you through your fears when you are afraid to win. He makes those who are weak strong. With His awesome power, you can do anything. You can go from good to great in ways that kept you thinking, 'I am good' but after tapping into His power, you found that you are great at what you do. There is nothing too hard for the Lord. He can use us when we are at our weakest point. He helps us when no one else can. That's God's awesome power.

Let us Pray:

Lord, thank you for reminding us of how awesome you are. Thank you for your wonderous working power in the precious blood of the Lamb.
In Jesus name. Amen

Song to Ponder: *Awesome God --Helen Baylor*

--Alma Jean Chambliss

Day Eleven

Describe a time you were at your weakest point, and God's awesome power took brought you through.

Day Twelve

Great Is Thy Faithfulness

Lamentations 3:23 New International Version (NIV)

23 They are new every morning: great is thy faithfulness.

As a young mother with a young child, God has always provided. I believe He provided for my journey as a mother fulfilling His promises for my purpose here on earth. With a young child at my side, He provided my education through college. Being far away from home for the first time alone, He provided a career as a software engineer with great protection. As always, He provided a roof over our heads, food on the table, adequate transportation, and supporting family and friends over the years. He has never forsaken me.

My prayer has always been with faith "God's going take care of Lisa and Dameion." That He keeps doing every day. His mercies are new every morning. Great is Thy faithfulness. I have the faith that He will provide. All I have needed; thy hands have provided with mercy and love. He gives me strength for today and hopes for the next. Each morning there are new mercies. His blessings have been all mine.

Now, fast forward to the future, the Lord keeps providing and taking care of us. With His everlasting love and mercy, He has provided for my son as a young man on the same journey fulfilling His promises.

Great is Thy faithfulness, Lord, unto me. So, keep the faith and keep holding on. God will provide because of His faithfulness to you.

Let us Pray:

Dear Heavenly Father. Thank you for your faithfulness. Thank you for your love and mercy every day of my life. Continue thy faithfulness unto me,
O Lord. Amen

Song to Ponder: *Great is Thy faithfulness – CeCe Winans*

--Arleathia Chambliss Wright

Day Twelve

How great has His faithfulness been for you?

Day Thirteen

Jesus Is The Great High Priest

Hebrews 4:12-16 New International Version (NIV)

12 For the word of God is alive and active. Sharper than any double-edged sword, it penetrates even to divide soul and spirit, joints and marrow; it judges the thoughts and attitudes of the heart. 13 Nothing in all creation is hidden from God's sight. Everything is uncovered and laid bare before the eyes of him to whom we must give account.

14 Therefore, since we have a great high priest who has ascended into heaven,[a] Jesus the Son of God, let us hold firmly to the faith we profess. 15 For we do not have a high priest who is unable to empathize with our weaknesses, but we have one who has been tempted in every way, just as we are—yet he did not sin. 16 Let us then approach God's throne of grace with confidence, so that we may receive mercy and find grace to help us in our time of need.

God's word is full of living power. The bible tells us that His word is sharper than a two-edge sword. It will either get you coming or going. It exposes us for who we are. We cannot hide anything from God. He sees all, and he knows all.

That is why we have a High Priest, who is Jesus Christ. It was necessary for him to become human like us so He could suffer and be tempted. The only difference is Jesus was without sin. Jesus knows what we go through each day, and He is qualified to help us when we are tempted. When you are tempted, think of what Jesus would do without sin. Then, trust in Him and He will see you through those temptations.

For all who come against us, Jesus is for us. He is the Most High who did not let people raddle is nerves causing him to curse them. We must not entertain those who are against us causing us to sin. We will be tempted, but do not sin.

So, go boldly to the throne of grace and obtain grace and mercy and find help when you need it. Because of what Jesus did on the cross, we can come to God through prayer anywhere and anytime.

Let us Pray:

Dear Father, thank you for sending Jesus here to earth to demonstrate His love and suffering on our behalf and being the Great High Priest. Thanks for knowing what we go through each day and giving us your grace and mercy to help us through. I
n Jesus name. Amen

Song to Ponder: *I will trust in the Lord. Baptist Hymn*

---Alma Jean Chambliss

Day Thirteen

Describe a time when Jesus helped you when you were tempted to sin.

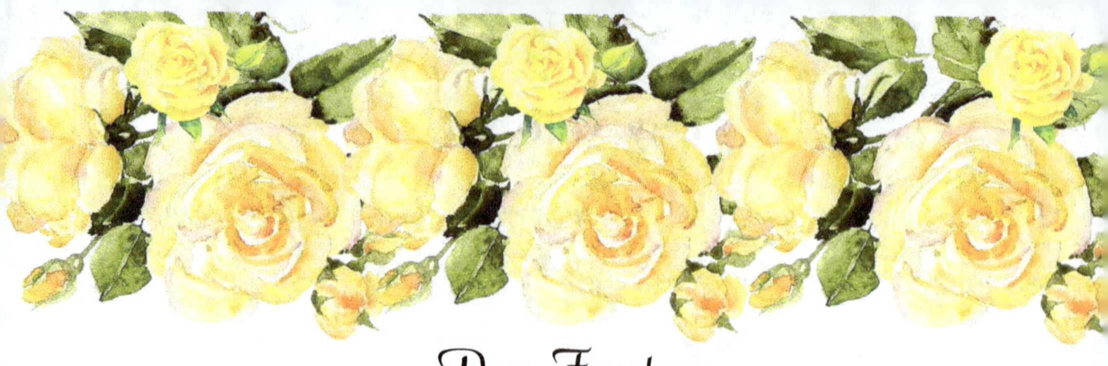

Day Fourteen

What He Requires

Read: Luke 9:23 New International Version (NIV)

23 Then he said to them all: "Whoever wants to be my disciple must deny themselves and take up their cross daily and follow me.

After sitting in the pews for several years in church, I began to scan the congregation and noticed that there were some worshipers I admired. These worshipers were glorifying and praising God through dance, praise, and song. They would cry and shout. There were those who were quoting scripture if not to themselves, they were reciting the scriptures as the pastor was quoting them verbatim. I would wonder what must have happened in their lives to enable them to worship the way they do. What is their story? Their testimony? Is it like mine or is it deeper than the next person?

I began to think that I was missing something. I would ask myself, why are you not quoting scriptures? Then, I asked the Lord, do I have to read the entire Bible to enable me to become a better worshipper? What do I need to do to learn Your Word? But then, I pondered whether I was ready to discover more about being a Christian even though I continue to believe that Christ died for my sins and accepted Christ as my savior.

I am fortunate to be a member of a church that offers discipleship courses to members and non-members of the church. After taking an assessment class to discover how to become a servant of the Lord in His Kingdom, I took my first discipleship class that changed my life as a Christian. My heart has always been in the right place credited to the spiritual foundation of my mother and grandmother. Immediately, I learned to confess to God, ask for forgiveness and to restore my heart. This was my prayer, "Lord, I want to be a better worshipper, praising and glorifying You. Lord, I want my heart to be committed to You and all that You do in my life; this way everyone will see it is what You do in my life and not me."

Since I made this commitment, I have decided to become a true disciple of Christ and build a lifelong, obedient relationship with Him. A disciple of Christ is someone who makes Christ Lord of his or her life. However, in order to become a disciple, in Luke 9:23, Jesus said unto them, "Whoever wants to be my disciple must deny himself, take up their cross daily and follow me". It is REQUIRED.I have set out to obey and do His will and will depend on Him to accomplish whatever He wants to accomplish in my life as best I can. I am not perfect, but this orchestrated the course of the rest of my life, and I am glad about it. Being a disciple for Christ has reassessed my stance in my relationship with Him. Now that I know what Jesus requires of me, I am no longer self-centered. I am willing to deny myself, take up my cross and follow Him, making Him priority in my life.

Let us Pray:

Father God, thank you for moving on my behalf
removing obstacles that were standing in my way.
You allowed the holy spirit to speak to me, reassessing
my thoughts to become a disciple for Christ. By
doing this, you have opened doors I could not have
opened myself. For this, I thank you.
In Jesus name, Amen.

Song to Ponder: *Church Hymn - At the cross*

--Arleathia Chambliss Wright

Day Fourteen

Are you ready to be a disciple for Christ? What will it take for you to meet Jesus' requirements?

Day Fifteen

Jesus Saves a Sinner

Luke 19:1-10 New International Version (NIV)

9 Jesus said to him, "Today salvation has come to this house, because this man, too, is a son of Abraham. 10 For the Son of Man came to seek and to save the lost."

The story is about Zacchaeus, a short, wealthy tax collector who climbed the sycamore tree to see Jesus over the crowd as He passed through Jericho. Jesus saw him and told Zacchaeus to come down out the tree because He was going to be a guest at his home. Zacchaeus was very excited and climbed down immediately. Zacchaeus was a sinner in need of a savior because of the way he stole from people. The people frowned at the fact Jesus was going to Zacchaeus house, of all people.

What if Jesus invited Himself to your house, would you be excited and joyful? What would people think of you? We should feel delighted when Jesus comes into our hearts. Many of us have degrees, good jobs, and nice things. Some of us have mistreated people to get where we are in life. Then when God wants to come into our life to save us from ourselves, we do not allow Him in. We need to learn to acknowledge that He is the one providing all that we have, even as a sinner. Then be excited that He invited himself to come into your home. The wealthiest man should not have so much that he will not invite Jesus in.

Jesus comes to save the lost while others judge them. He would even visit a thief, a killer, and a liar. He does this because Jesus loves everyone, like He loved Zacchaeus. Jesus granted him salvation. That visit changed Zacchaeus' heart as a sinner. When we allow Jesus in, we will change our ways as a sinner as well. He will save us and make our crooked places straight. So do not be so quick to judge a sinner.

Let us Pray:

Thank you, Lord, for saving us. You know that we are sinners and saved us anyway. There are so many others o ut there who need the good news of salvation. Touch each of them right now and save them.
In Jesus name. Amen

Song to Ponder: *You are the Only One – Kirk Franklin*

--Alma Jean Chambliss

Day Fifteen

Describe a time when Jesus came into your heart and saved you.

Day Sixteen

Nothing Is Too Hard

Read: Genesis 18:13-14 New International Version (NIV)

14 Is anything too hard for the Lord? I will return to you at the appointed time next year, and Sarah will have a son."

I remember when I bought my first home. My son and I had moved to the big City of Atlanta to the Metropolitan area called Decatur. We lived with the sister of a very close friend of the family and her daughter in a two-bedroom apartment. She was so kind to open her home and give up her daughter's room to my son and me. I was working 3rd shift at Federal Express until I could find a job in my career to afford my own apartment.

Once I was blessed with the job in my field, I was preparing to look for my own apartment. As I was searching for a place for my son and I, the rent payment for a two-bedroom apartment was so expensive. I reflected on the amount I paid when I lived in Alabama. I became afraid that I would not be able to afford a place in Atlanta and would have to stay with my friend a lot longer than I anticipated.

I began to think, "Lord, I am 28 years old, a single mother, just starting a new job, no family around and the cost of living is way too high to invest in a home." I was thinking "no way". It seemed unlikely. "What if I fail, not being able to pay the mortgage each month, keeping up the maintenance of a house, etc." This was a huge step that did not seem possible. Then the holy spirit spoke to my spirit telling me that my son would have a backyard to play in, unlike an apartment; he would play with the neighborhood kids; when my family comes to visit, they would have their own room; a great starter home as a young single mother.

I began to believe what the Lord said to Abraham that there was nothing too hard for the Lord. That, yes, it looks impossible, but God can do the impossible. I told myself to just trust Him and remove all fears. God is going to take care of me and my son. He holds the future. Little did we know that our family friends were a part of a plan that the LORD was orchestrating. The Lord blessed me with a starter home three-bedroom/two-bathroom affordable home. The blessing was more than enough, and more than I asked for. Whatever looks impossible in your life, if it is God's purpose for you, he will start it and he will finish it. Know that the promise He brings to you as He did for me, will come to pass. I know the Lord will make a way. Oh yes, He will. There's nothing too hard for Jesus.

Let us Pray:

Father God, thank you for being a blessing to me.
Thank you for orchestrating your plan when I did
not believe I could do things on my own. I know now
that all things are possible through you, and
nothing is too hard for you. I pray to always
seek you first in all things.
In Jesus name I pray. Amen.

Song to Ponder: *I know the Lord will make a way – Smokie Norful*

--Arleathia Chambliss Wright

Day Sixteen

Have there been anything that you thought was too hard for you, but not for the Lord?

Day Seventeen

They That Wait

Read: Isaiah 40:31 New International Version (NIV)

But those who wait on the Lord
Shall renew their strength;
They shall mount up with wings like eagles,
They shall run and not be weary,
They shall walk and not faint.

God wants us to live the best life possible. If we are willing to follow him, he will show us the way. Trust Him and wait. There are ways to experience life to the fullest. First, we must put our trust in God, read God's word each day, pray without ceasing, and put him first in everything you do. When a person discovers God is a real glorious being, they find out that it is God who is the answer to all our troubles. So, wait on the Lord and He will renew your strength.

Have you waited on him for anything? I know there are a lot of things that I did not wait on the Lord for. I have made purchases and accepted jobs without waiting for Him. I would pray first seeking Him, but in my mind, He was taking longer than I expected. However, when I went forward without waiting on Him, I suffered harsh consequences. When I realized my move was not the best move, I started to wait on Him to renew my strength, giving me patience to endure.

We do not get all we want all the time, but we get exactly what God wants us to have. In some ways, we act like children. Whenever we see what we want, we want it right away. We think we should have it. Let us practice waiting on the Lord. He will give us all that we need and more. No matter what, good things happen to you if you trust God first.

Let us Pray:

Dear God, thank you God for renewing my strength in all my struggles. Each day you wake me up I want to put you first waiting and trusting you with everything I need. In Jesus Holy name. Amen.

Song to Ponder: *They that Wait – Fred Hammond*

--Alma Jean Chambliss

Day Seventeen

Describe a time you waited on the Lord to renew your strength.

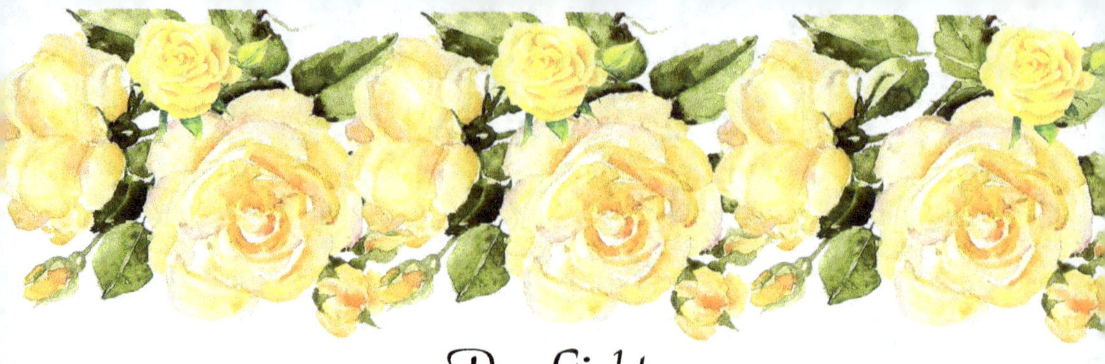

Day Eighteen

The Solid Rock

Read: Matthew 7:24-27 New International Version (NIV)

24 "Therefore everyone who hears these words of mine and puts them into practice is like a wise man who built his house on the rock. 25 The rain came down, the streams rose, and the winds blew and beat against that house; yet it did not fall, because it had its foundation on the rock. 26 But everyone who hears these words of mine and does not put them into practice is like a foolish man who built his house on sand. 27 The rain came down, the streams rose, and the winds blew and beat against that house, and it fell with a great crash."

Have you heard what Jesus talks about in Matthew 5:45? He states, "for He makes His sun rise on evil and good and sends rain on the just and the unjust." What does this mean to you? It means that being a faithful servant (good; the just) does not exempt you from the storms of life. You will have some storms, hardships, and bumps in the road. We also see this happening to an unfaithful servant (evil; the unjust) or people who just do not believe in God. It is harder for an unfaithful man to go through the storms and difficulties. Why? Because they do not know where their help comes from. But you, as a faithful servant, know that your help comes from the Lord.

Jesus also speaks in Matthew 7:24-27 about a wise man who built his house on solid rock. He honored God. But there was another man who foolishly built his house out of sand and did not honor God. When the rain descended, storms with floods came, and winds blew on the houses, the storm calmed leaving the house on solid rock standing. The house built of sand was blown down.

We all try to do things our own way that is not solid enough to stand. The decisions we have made have put us further behind, in a bind, and nowhere to turn. So, let your hope be built on nothing less than Jesus' blood and righteousness. Jesus Christ is solid as a rock. Anything else is sinking sand. He sends the rain for us all, but the one who believes, will not fall.

Let us pray:

Father God in Heaven, how precious is thy name. As we honor you, we are standing on the solid rock believing we will not fall. Our hope is built on nothing less than Jesus' blood and righteousness. We pray for the unjust that they look to you to carry them through. For all other ground is sinking sand.
In Jesus name, Amen.

Song to Ponder: *Solid Rock -- an old spiritual hymn by Edward Mote*

--Arleathia Chambliss Wright

Day Eighteen

What have you tried to do on your own that wasn't solid enough to stand?

Day Nineteen

Obey & Love The Lord

Read: Deuteronomy 6:5 New International Version (NIV)

5You shall love the Lord your God with all your heart, with all your soul, and with all your strength.

Obey and love the Lord your God. He loves you. Why is it taking so long for you to GET IT? I have come to realize that some will, and most will not. This reminds me of the people of Israel who wandered day and night for 40 years in a hot desert because they could not figure it out. A lot of them died trying to figure it out. They missed out 40 years earlier. But this time, Moses made it clear about God's promise. In Deuteronomy 3, he said to them that when you are careful to obey, life will be well for you, and you will have a surge in the land of flowing milk and honey. If this is more than you have now, why not? The only conditions were to obey and love the Lord.

The fifth verse, says we shall "love the Lord our God with all your heart, with all your soul and with all your strength." Moses said these commandments must be in your heart. Teach this commandment to your children so that it will stay on their minds growing up. Because if it is in their hearts, they will always remember. Surround you and your family with His word. This helps to build a foundation in your heart for life. You will never forget who He is.

My children went to Sunday School and church. They attended mission meetings and vacation bible school. Then when their children came along, they made sure their children were raised in church and attended faith-based schools. The best way to effectively learn the eternal truths is in a loving God-fearing home. Make a daily commitment to see God in all aspects in life. So, do all that you can, and learn to obey and love the Lord. He commands it. Try Him and see.

Let us Pray:

Lord, help me to remember that you love me, and I should love you as well. Teach me your word embedding your word in my heart. I want to teach my family and those around me in my actions how to obey and love you. Please search my heart and remove anything that is not pleasing to you.
In Jesus name. Amen

Song to Ponder: *Obey Anyway – Brian Courtney Wilson*

--Alma Jean Chambliss

Day Nineteen

Describe a time you have obeyed and told the Lord you love Him.

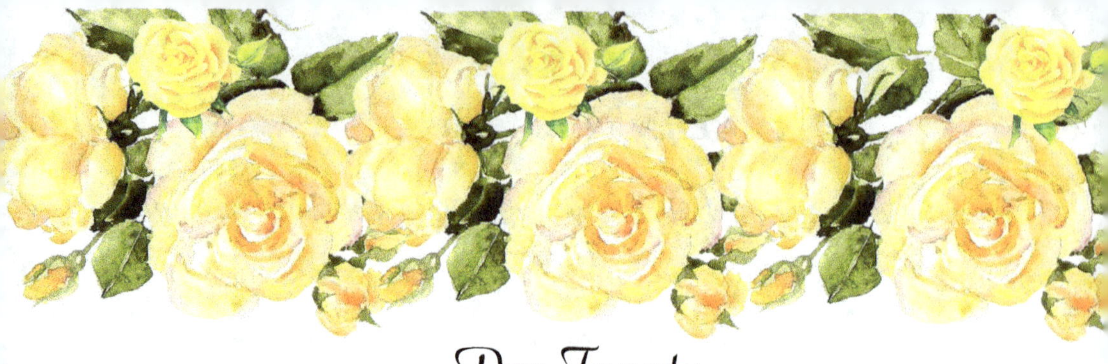

Day Twenty

We Delight Ourselves

Psalm 112: 1-2 New International Version (NIV)

1 Praise the Lord.[b]

Blessed are those who fear the Lord,
who find great delight in his commands.

2 Their children will be mighty in the land;
the generation of the upright will be blessed.

Scripture says, happy are those who fear the Lord. Yes, happy are those who delight in doing His commands.

My mom and grandmother are the people to thank for the love, kindness, and generosity my sisters and brother show towards people. We have been raised on the foundation of knowing Christ Jesus, having faith, loving one another, and doing what is right as God commands us.

We are delighted in knowing the Lord. We began to know Him through our mother and grandmother who were instrumental in the church and in the study of His Word. They kept us involved in church to learn His commands. They taught us that we had to build a personal relationship with him in order to trust Him. Happy are those who delight in doing His commands. We are delighted.

Having much faith in His word, we began to do what was right as best we can and what was fair according to his commands. We delight ourselves in helping others in need. When we help people in need, it does not necessarily involve money. Believe it or not, when calling, visiting, giving, and praying for someone with a simple gesture of kindness is all most people need to make it through the day. When we believe that God is pleased with our act of kindness, it makes us happy.

So, make your decisions based on generosity, love & kindness, then many blessings will come to you and your children. Then you will be delighted in Him as well.

Let us Pray:

Father God in heaven, we thank you for blessing our family. We delight in Your commands as best we can. Thank you for building a strong foundation through our mother and grandmother. We ask these and other blessings in Your name. Amen

Song to Ponder: *Again I say Rejoice – Israel and New Breed*

--Arleathia Chambliss Wright

Day Twenty

Do you find great delight in His commands?

Day Twenty-One

People Showing Kindness

Read: Matthew 10:42 New International Version (NIV)

42 And if anyone gives even a cup of cold water to one of these little ones who is my disciple, truly I tell you, that person will certainly not lose their reward."

The bible tells us that if you give even a cup of cold water to one of the least of my followers, you will surely be rewarded. Jesus used this example of giving water to a thirsty child as a model of unselfish service.

I believe in my heart that showing love and kindness is my calling. I love people and I do not mind helping those who cannot help themselves. The Lord tells us to be loving and kind to His people. The people who do not have compassion for God's people, are the people who are always against others. People who love God, determines how they will treat other people.

It is just nice to be nice. When you see someone in need, let the spirit lead you to give. There is no harm in helping if you do not have a hidden motive to do so. God loves a cheerful giver no matter how big or little the gesture is.

I have had a lot of help from people showing kindness to me as well. So many people were there for me when I needed help with my handicapped child. They provided gas money and transportation for rides to the doctor appointments. I will appreciate those people for the rest of my life. God will surely reward them for doing so. He notices every good deed.

Let us Pray:

Thank you, God, for those people who always show kindness to me even when I was taking care of my daughter. You said, it pleases you when people show kindness, and they will be rewarded for doing so.
In Jesus name I pray. Amen

Song to Ponder: *I need you to survive. -- Hezekiah Walker and The Love Fellowship Choir*

--Alma Jean Chambliss

Day Twenty-One

Describe a time where you have shown kindness for someone and God rewarded you dearly.

Day Twenty-Two

Be Selective

Read: Proverbs 22:24 – 25 New International Version (NIV)

24 Do not make friends with a hot-tempered person,
do not associate with one easily angered,
25 or you may learn their ways
and get yourself ensnared.

Have you ever been told that if you hang around successful people, you will be successful and if you hang around unsuccessful people, you may become unsuccessful? These expressions determine the winners and losers. I have found this statement to be so true.

Scripture says, "Do not make friends with a hot-tempered person, do not associate with one easily angered, or you may learn their ways and get yourself ensnared." If you are hanging out with the wrong crowd, these types of people are unhappy, negative, always critical, cannot get ahead, getting into trouble, making excuses for everything, finding fault, and blaming others for their mistakes. When you encounter a relationship with these types of people, put on your best pair of sneakers and run like hell. Remember, misery loves company. The negative things they are doing can easily rub off on you. These people are not for you. They will pull you into their environment and people will not want to hang out with you. If those are not your qualities, it is okay to be selective of who you hang around.

If you want to be successful, you hang around successful people. You know this because God has given you --- your gifts and character that no one else can take away from you. Your assignment is to be great, fulfilling His purpose. Be selective. To reach your highest potential, you must surround yourself around eagles who soar, people who make you happy, who value your worth, who bring the best out of you. God produces eagles. Stop settling for the wrong crowd and be a part of His plan and protect what God has entrusted you with.

Let us Pray:

Father God, thank you for giving us the ok to be selective. Thank you for your hedge of protection around us as we surround ourselves around people. Thank you for giving us the discernment to know when to be selective without judgement and knowing that you help to protect us so we can reach our highest potential around successful and positive people.
In Jesus name, we pray. Amen

Song to Ponder: *A Friend – The Winans*

--Arleathia Chambliss Wright

Day Twenty-Two

When was a time you had to 'Be Selective' of some people you hung out with or decisions you had to make?

Day Twenty-Three

Do You know God?

Read: Joshua 1:8 New International Version (NIV)

8 This Book of the Law shall not depart from your mouth, but you[a] shall meditate in it day and night, that you may observe to do according to all that is written in it. For then you will make your way prosperous, and then you will have good success.

God is your Creator. He created the heaven and the earth. He created human beings in his own image giving us the breath of life. He is the living God who died then arose. He is our Father; we are His children. God provides for us. Everything we have is from Him. He is Peace. His peace passes all understanding. If you do not know him, you better try Him.

So many people are missing out on what God intends for us. He intends for us to have a life-long obedient relationship with Him and promises abundant life. We only call upon Him when we are in trouble and living according to our own standards. We are making a mess of things.

The bible says that we cannot know Him and his ways until we are born again. 1 John 1:9 states that we must repent of our sins and yield to the Lord. He will forgive us and cleanse us from all unrighteousness. This is the only way we can personally relate to God. Paul said in 1 Corinthians 2:14, "But the person without the Spirit does not accept the things that come from the Spirit of God but considers them foolishness and cannot understand them because they are discerned only through the Spirit."

The first step to knowing and hearing from God is to repent of your sins and trust Him as your Lord and Savior. Then you will have full knowledge of Him and His standards.

Read the bible daily and meditate on his word day and night. Joshua 1:8 declares for us to "keep this Book of the Law always on your lips; meditate day and night, so that you may be careful to do everything written in it. Then you will be prosperous and successful."

So, let's read his word every day so that we can get to know him. He is there waiting. All you need to do is call Him. Isn't it wonderful that we can call him anytime? We are nothing without Him.

Let us Pray:

Heavenly Father, I want to get to know you. Teach me your Word as I meditate on them. Clean my mind and h eart removing all that is not pleasing to you Lord. In Jesus name. Amen.

Song to Ponder: *Nothing Without You – Smokie Norful*

--Alma Jean Chambliss

Day Twenty-Three

Describe some things about the Lord that you have studied and mediated on.

Day Twenty-Four

Too Busy For Jesus

Read: Luke 10:41- 42 New King James Version (NKJV)

41 And [a]Jesus answered and said to her, "Martha, Martha, you are worried and troubled about many things. 42 But one thing is needed, and Mary has chosen that good part, which will not be taken away from her."

Do you think serving the Lord is the only time you need to spend with Him? Some people think that attending church on Sundays, being a part of all the auxiliaries, and holding a position for all the special events at church is spending time with the Lord. Some people get caught up doing religious practices other than spiritually commit to God. We also get caught up in our careers and major accomplishments and forget to acknowledge him. We often think because we attend church or religious events having to do with Him, is good enough to acknowledge and thank him.

When I found some time to spend with the Lord, I read what Jesus said to Martha in Luke 10:38-42 where Martha welcomed Jesus and his disciples into her home. Martha was so busy preparing dinner and doing for others, she had no time for Jesus. Her sister, Mary, on the other hand, sat at Jesus feet and listened to what Jesus had to say. Martha was so aggravated about Mary not helping her, she mentions this to Jesus. Jesus had an unexpected response. He told Martha she needed to be more concerned about, basically, what He had to say, and He was not going to take that moment from her sister. Jesus told Martha that she was "worried and troubled about many things". He is saying, you are doing too much. I just need you to sit still and acknowledge me.

Let's be careful not to let our service or careers become busy work and self-serving. Getting caught up in the world causes us to be too busy for the Lord. Jesus does not want us to stop serving but asking that we set our priorities. Take some time out to spend time with the Master. He will lighten your load and give your life a balance.

Let Us Pray:

Dear heavenly father, thank you for showing how we are preoccupied instead of being spiritually committed. Lord, I ask that you help me to prioritize my schedule to spend more time with you. As your servant, Lord, we must realize that we must sit still and listen to You. For listening to You, will lighten our load for sure. In Jesus name, Amen.

Songs to Ponder: *Never too busy – Byron Cage*

--Arleathia Chambliss Wright

Day Twenty-Four

In what ways do you spend your time with the Master?

Day Twenty-Five

Turn From The Error Of Your Ways

Read: Ezekiel 18:4 New International Version (NIV)

4 For everyone belongs to me, the parent as well as the child—both alike belong to me. The one who sins, is the one who will die.

We are all personally responsible for our own sins we commit. We cannot blame anyone else for the wrong that we have done or are still doing. Yes, someone may have played a part in the sinful behavior, but you are ultimately responsible if you do not confess and turn from your wicked ways.

The people of Judah thought that they were being punished for the sins of their ancestors. For the ancestors who were righteous, they thought they would live and not be punished. Ezekiel, a prophet of God, told them to repent of their sins. He warned that the one that sin would surely die. If we do good and what is pleasing to God, we will live.

If we remain righteous and do what is right like not serving other gods, committing adultery, mistreating, and stealing from others, we will live. And if we have a loved one who is doing all these things, and we decide to do the same, the punishment will be for both of us individually because God judges everyone individually. We are held accountable for our own actions.

Begin to turn from the error of your ways and do not let your sin destroy you.

Let us Pray:

Thank you, Father, for saving me. Thanks for hearing my prayer. Please forgive me for the things that are not pleasing to you. Please turn me from the error of my ways and let your will be done.
In Jesus name. Amen.

Song to Ponder: *Sinners Prayer – Deitrick Haddon*

--Alma Jean Chambliss

Day Twenty-Five

Describe something you continuously do and need help from God to walk away from.

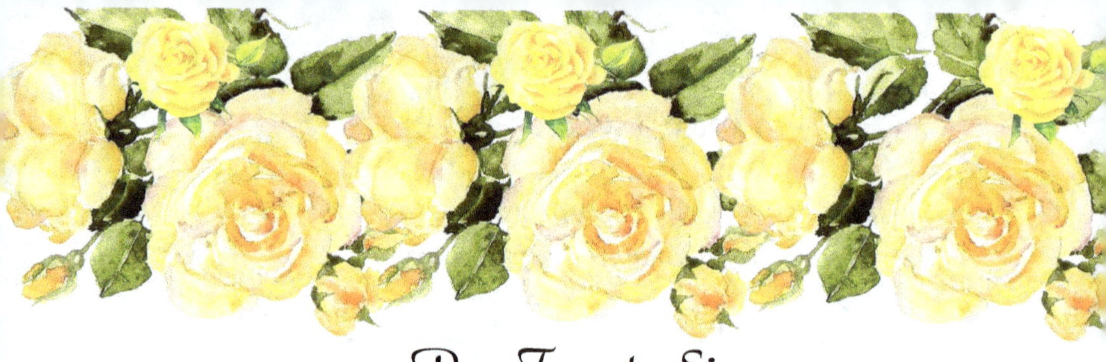

Day Twenty-Six

Covered By The Blood

Read: Psalm 91:11 New International Version (NIV)

For He will command His angels concerning you to guard you in all your ways.

Well, it's true what they say, "You have to drive for yourself and everyone else".

I have been in two close calls for car accidents that I can remember. When I tell you that I am 'covered by the Blood', you betcha! What was meant to kill me, God step in and said no. After witnessing the power of the Holy Spirit, I am convinced.

The first incident was a car heading towards me head on sitting at a traffic light. The holy spirit stepped in and the passenger in the car with the driver grabbed the wheel to keep the driver from hitting me. Fast forward, another incident where I was leaving a split mall approaching a GREEN light. As I proceed to drive through the intersection, the holy spirit told me to look to my left as I approached the middle of the intersection. I looked to the left and there was a car coming towards me. In a quick second, I was confused thinking I was in the wrong and maybe I am the one running a RED light. However, immediately, as I looked up at my GREEN light, an angel pressed the accelerator as the car just missed me running the RED light not realizing it until they actually drove through the RED light. The car would have T-Boned me with damage and injury to the both of us. But Glory be to God.

As I turn to the left to proceed home, I immediately Praised the Lord and thanked HIM for protecting me. Psalm 91:11 saids, For He will command His angels concerning you to guard you in all your ways. I gave the Lord credit for dispatching his angels to save me and admitted to Him that I am covered by His Blood in Jesus name. Acknowledge your encounters today because you too, are covered by the blood of Jesus. Then, thank him for his grace and mercy that protected you.

Your faith in God as your Protector should bring you through all threats with no scratches or bruises. Surrender your fears to him with faith in Him no matter what. In order to do this, you must always dwell in Him.

Let us pray:

Father God, thank you for interceding on my behalf.
You commanded your angels concerning me to guard
me during my time of need. For that, I thank you
and I am forever grateful to you.
In Jesus name, Amen.

Song to Ponder: *Jesus Be a Fence around me. – Fred Hammond*

--Arleathia Chambliss Wright

Day Twenty-Six

Can you recall an encounter where the Lord dispatched his angels to guard you?

Day Twenty-Seven

How To Build a Relationship With God

Read: John 8:31-32 & John 15: 7 New International Version (NIV)

31 To the Jews who had believed him, Jesus said, "If you hold to my teaching, you are really my disciples. 32 Then you will know the truth, and the truth will set you free."

7 If you remain in me and my words remain in you, ask whatever you wish, and it will be done for you.

Building a relationship with God is a two-way communication, reading His word and praying with faith.

First, God speaks to us through the bible. In order us to get to know Him, we must read His word. In His word, He tells us all about Himself. In John 8:31-32, Jesus said to the Jews who had believed Him, "If you hold to my teaching, you are really my disciples. Then you will know the truth, and the truth will set you free." While reading a bible verse, ask yourself what this means. He wants you to not only read His word but hold on to His teachings and the promises His word gives to us. By doing this you will know the truth for yourself, and you will be free. Being free is the freedom of understanding what the Father promised you in His word. His love is freedom.

I always read scripture over many times. I read the verses before and after it. Then, I write it down when I began to understand what I am reading. The more I read the verse, the more I understand it. The Holy Spirit can change your thoughts, your speech, and your behavior as you read to help you understand. We need to allow God to use the principles in His word to build our relationship with Him.

Second, praying with faith is when you go to God in prayer believing that His word that you have read is true. In John 15:7 Jesus said, "If you remain in me and my words remain in you, ask whatever you wish, and it will be done for you." Ask him to give you an understanding of what the word is saying, and the Holy Spirit will help you. As the songwriter suggests, we are 'standing on the promises of God'. Therefore, you are getting to know Him through his word, with the understanding from the Holy Spirit. This will help you to have a conversation with Him when you pray building that relationship.

So, start building a relationship with God today, by standing on the promises of God that will set you free.

Let us Pray:

Father God, thank you for your promises. I come to you today standing on the promises I desperately need. I am open to building a relationship to learn what those promises are for me.
In Jesus name I pray Amen.

Song to Ponder: *Standing on the Promises of God*

--Alma Jean Chambliss

Day Twenty-Seven

Describe ways you communicate with God that helps you build a obedient relationship with Him.

Day Twenty-Eight

Feeling Distress

Read: Matthew 26: 39 New King James Version (NKJV)

39 He went a little farther and fell on His face, and prayed, saying, "O My Father, if it is possible, let this cup pass from Me; nevertheless, not as I will, but as You will."

Have you heard of the time when Jesus was in distress? During His final moments before the crucifixion, Jesus was in distress. Judas agreed to betray Jesus and Jesus predicts Peter's denial. Think about it. Jesus hung out with the 12 disciples performing miracles and saving lives, then some of them decide to go against him. On top of that, he was carrying the thoughts of being crucified. This really exposes Jesus emotional state of mind. So, Jesus went to God in prayer.

Jesus went to God in prayer three times to request the Lord to 'take this cup from Me'. The 'cup' was all the events that caused His distress. He did not stop there. He said to God, 'let thy will be done'. He said, Father, if it is Your will that I go through this? Then let Your will be done and not my own. He taught this prayer to his disciples in the Disciple's Prayer-The Lord's Prayer. We as Christians have memorized the same words as we pray, let thy will be done.

Imagine going through a situation that has you in distress and your only refuge is to go to God. You may become distressed about someone betraying you, denying you, divorcing you, or passing away. But, the first thing you decide is to do your own will, and make the biggest mess of the situation. You go to confront the person filled with anger, or lie in bed crying day and night over it. Then you do not understand why you cannot get out of the situation or overcome what has happened. Lean not unto your own understanding. Go to him in prayer, requesting that he take this cup from you and let God's will be done.

God's will is not always our will and vice versa. God's will for us to do one thing, and we turn around and do another. That means you do not trust his will. We should trust his will more than our own. Imagine, if Jesus was in distress by these things. Then, we will be in distress by the trials and tribulations in our lives as well. We just need to remember the steps he took to make it through His distress. Amen, Praise the Lord.

Let us Pray:

Dear heavenly father, we come to you during our time of need. I am feeling distress Lord. Please take this cup from me Lord. Let thy will be done. I trust you and will keep the faith that you will remove all obstacles in my way of serving you.
In Jesus name I pray. Amen.

Song to Ponder: *In Your Will – Men of Standard*

--Arleathia Chambliss Wright

Day Twenty-Eight

Name a time you were in distress. What did you do to get through your distress?

Day Twenty-Nine

Safe In His Arms

Read: Isaiah 40:10 New King James Version (NKJV)

Behold, the Lord God shall come [a]with a strong hand,
And His arm shall rule for Him;
Behold, His reward is with Him,
And His [b]work before Him.

The good news is for us to put all our trust in God because He cares for us. He will go to bat for us. Because of His power and authority, we need to know that He still loves us, supplies our needs, and wants to protect us like a Shepard who watches over His sheep.

My house has been through three fires. I have escape all three unharmed, safe in his arms.

He tells us in His word that when the storms of life are raging, He will never leave us or forsake us. So, believe in His word when he says you are safe in His arms. God is a God who does not lie. We can count on Him. In the world we are living in has violence and killings. We need to trust God wholeheartedly finding strength and security in Him.

Because the Lord is our Shepard, we have everything we need. The Lord has died for us so one day we will have eternal life. Let us trust Him and know that we are safe in His arms.

Let us Pray:

Dear God, we honor you today for all you have done. Thanks for keeping us safe in your arms so that we may have eternal life and spend the rest of our life with you. In Jesus mighty name. Amen

Song to Ponder: *Safe in His Arms – Rev Milton Brunson & the Thompson Community Singers*

--Alma Jean Chambliss

Day Twenty-Nine

Describe a situation when you knew you were safe in His Arms.

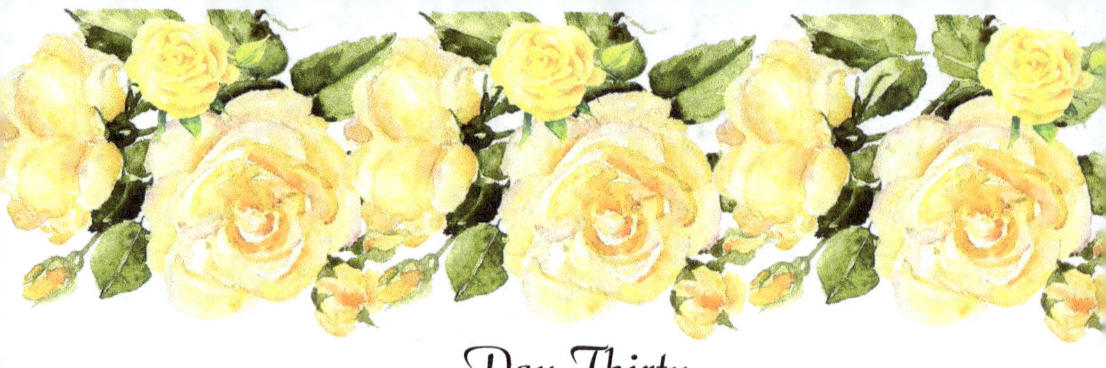

Day Thirty

In His Hands

Read: John 10:29 New International Version (NIV)

"I give them eternal life, and they shall never perish; no one will snatch them out of my hand. My Father, who has given them to me, is greater than all; no one can snatch them out of my Father's hand."

Do you remember the song, "He's got the world in his hand"? As a little girl, we would sing this song in youth fellowship. At that time as a little one, we believed in what the teachers said, that God had the whole world in his hand and that he would take care of the whole world. As an adult, this is still true. During difficult times, he has kept me and continues to keep me in his hand. Not just during those dark times, but during good times as well.

When I was laid off longer than the first time, I prayed each day for a job. I would network with others to see if they knew of any openings. Then it got so bad that no one was calling for interviews and no one was hiring. When I thought I had run out of prayers, I remembered my pastor saying just call out his name. I cried out JESUS, JESUS, JESUS! I surrender all to you.

Jesus began to speak to me. "Have I ever failed you? Have you lost your house; the roof over your head? Have your lights been turned off, power for your stove? Is food on the table; for you and your son to eat? Has the car been repossessed; to use to look for the job and go on interviews?"

God said, "if I did it before, I'll do it again. No one can snatch you from My hands. Don't be discouraged. You've seen My mercies time and time again." He blows your mind every time. This does not stop the plans God has for you. No one or nothing can snatch you out of His hand. He is in control. You are in the palm of his hand.

Tell yourself, I am the child of the Most High God who is greater than them all. I am in his hand and cannot be snatched away. He knows when the time comes for me to start receiving phone calls for interviews and what company is best for me to fulfill his purpose. Bam! A fortune 100/500 company calls for an interview. You get the job with this company to which you have never applied for. So sit back. You are not alone. He has got the whole world in his hand.

Let us Pray

God, you are the Most High God. The one who is greater than them all. Thank you for having me in your hands where nothing can snatch me out. Thank you for your mercy once and again. In Jesus name. Amen

Song to ponder: *He has his hands on you. – Marvin Sapp*

--Arleathia Chambliss Wright

Day Thirty

Name a time you realized that God had you in the palm of his hands.

Day Thirty-One

God Will Strengthen Us

Read: Isaiah 41: 10 New International Version (NIV)

So do not fear, for I am with you;
do not be dismayed, for I am your God.
I will strengthen you and help you;
I will uphold you with my righteous right hand.

No matter what we are going through, God will strengthen us. God said he has all power in His hands. Believe it. In Isaiah 41:10, God tells us "Do not fear, for I am with you." That means to not worry or have anxiety, He is with you. And do not be discouraged, because He is your God.

No matter how big the situation is, no matter how impossible the odds may seem, God assures us that He will give us strength to endure and help us along the way. Glory to God. This is good news. No matter how long we live on this earth, hardship and heartbreaks will come. These hardships and heartbreaks can be a troubled relationship, loss of a loved one, unemployment, financial distress, and failing health. Whatever the case may be, He said he will uphold us with His righteous right hand.

Keep the faith and keep holding on. Please believe that He is upholding you in the midst of your storm. He will give you strength and help you see it through.

Let us Pray:

Father God, thank you for giving me strength to make it through my storm. Please keep reminding us that you are all we need. Especially when we are going through hardships and heart breaks. Thank you for upholding me with your righteous right hand. You are an awesome God. Thanks for being my God. In Jesus precious name Amen.

Song to Ponder: *Love Lifted Me – Spiritual Hymn*

--Alma Jean Chambliss

Day Thirty-One

Describe a time when you knew it was God who strengthen you.

Day Thirty-Two

Touch The Hem Of His Garment

Read: Mark 5:28 New International Version (NIV)

When she heard about Jesus, she came up behind him in the crowd and touched his cloak, 28 because she thought, "If I just touch his clothes, I will be healed. 29 Immediately her bleeding stopped, and she felt in her body that she was freed from her suffering."

I am reminded of the story of a woman of faith who was healed by Jesus with just a touch of his clothing, 'the helm of his garment.' The woman had been sick for twelve years with a flow of blood. This caused much sufferings because she spent all her money going from doctor to doctor looking for a cure or some help of some sort which leads to her running out of money. She never could find any help.

One day she heard Jesus was in town and joined the people who were following Him. She slips through the crowd to get close to Jesus. As she reached for Him, she thought, 'if I can just touch the helm of his garment, surely I will be healed.' Once she touched Jesus, immediately, the power of His healing, healed her body and she was made whole with no more bleeding. Hallelujah!

We all have some circumstances or crisis that we go through in life where we would like to just hear a word from Jesus, feel a touch from

Jesus or be in position to even touch the hem of his garment, and everything would be ok. We may face years' worth of financial debt, children on the wrong path, additions, joblessness, and illnesses. We have spent money that we had to rob Peter to pay Paul, bailing your children or spouse out of trouble, catering to additions, and going from doctor to doctor to get the best healthcare or not even having insurance to pay for your illness.

Let's keep our faith that God has the power to heal, clear debt, right wrongs, straighten paths, to deliver from additions when you call on his name or by touching the hem of his garment.

Let us Pray:

Father, let me touch you to see if you are real. If I can touch the hem of your garment, I know I will be made whole. I believe in your power Jesus. I have seen it time and time again. Thank you, Father. In Jesus name, Amen.

Song to Ponder: *Let me touch you – Kirk Franklin*

--Arleathia Chambliss Wright

Day Thirty-Two

What are some circumstances or crisis that you have gone through in life where you thought, "if I could just hear a Word from the Lord, or touch the helm of His garment, I would be okay?

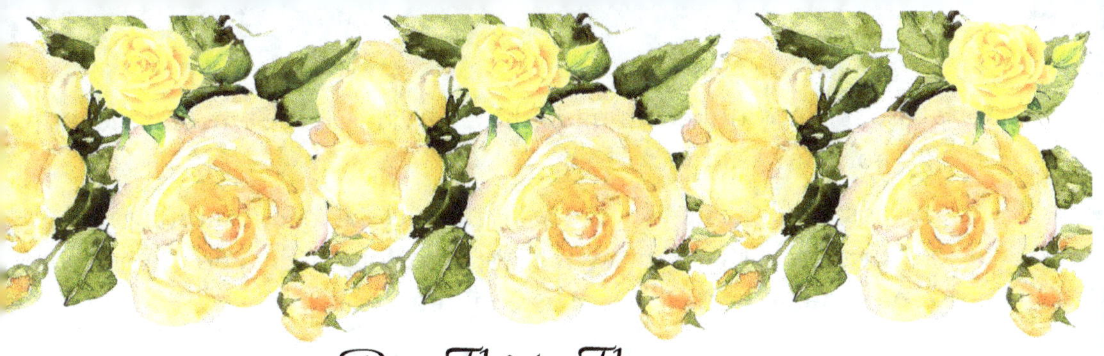

Day Thirty-Three

A Faithful Servant

Read: 2 Timothy 4:7 New International Version (NIV)

7 I have fought the good fight, I have finished the race, I have kept the faith.

A great example of being a faithful servant is Paul the Apostle. Paul was faithful and believed in Christ Jesus until his death. Paul traveled bringing the good news to the world as an evangelist and missionary preaching and teaching the gospel about Jesus. He reminds Timothy to keep the faith, the battle is already won. Stay in the fight to pursue God's will.

We may start out being faithful but get distracted by this world. For example, we may be a member of an auxiliary. We are dedicated to that position for some time, but then allow the enemy to make us feel bad about our dedication to the Lord. Now, unless you have a hidden motive to use that platform for mistreating others or for evil intent, then you are not being a faithful servant. A faithful servant is one who is committed to doing the Lord's work with faith, hope, and love. When you are committed to doing His work with enthusiasm and love, he will greatly reward you. Finish the race by keeping the faith.

The good news is that we still have a chance. We have a chance to do what's right, turn everything over to God, and let him lead and tell us what we should be doing as his servants. When we learn more about him, we can communicate with other believers and become witnesses for those in need of becoming faithful servants too. Someone must do it, why not you? God picked you.

So, let's spread the news about Jesus the Messiah being faithful servants of the Lord so that we can say that we have fought the good fight as we finish our course here on earth as Paul did.

Let us Pray:

Dear Lord, I want to be Your faithful servant. I want to spread the news about your son Jesus Christ. I pray for your guidance on how to be a good and faithful servant like Paul.
In Jesus name I pray Amen.

Song to Ponder: *Well Done – Detrick Haddon*

--Alma Jean Chambliss

Day Thirty-Three

Describe a situation you kept your faith and hung in there with God.

Day Thirty-Four

God Is My Help

Psalm 94:15-17 New International Version (NIV)

15 For what is decided will be right and good. And all those whose hearts are right will follow it. 16 Who will rise up for me against the sinful? Who will take a stand for me against those who do wrong? 17 If the Lord had not been my help, my soul would soon have been among the dead.

How many times have we heard, 'I lift my eyes to the hills from which comes my help; My help comes from you Lord.'? God is my help, my present help. When I go to him, he decides what is right and good. If your heart is right, you will follow what he decides.

Have you ever been in a situation where you followed what God says to your heart? There was a time that I had the opportunity to do wrong, but God stepped in. Not thinking clearly before my actions, God found a way to rise and stand against the enemy. The enemy who tried to pull me in the wrong direction, God stepped in. The enemy who told me that doing drugs was okay, God stepped in. The enemy who came to steal my joy, God stepped in. When the enemy said I couldn't, God said I could.

If it had not been for the Lord on my side, rising and standing up for me, I could have or would have been dead. What He decided was right and good for me. And because my heart is in the right place, I follow him. Glory to God.

Let us Pray:

Father God. Thank you for your grace and mercy that you were on my side Lord. You are my help, my present help.
In Jesus name. Amen

Song to Ponder: *All of my help comes from the Lord. – Hezekiah Walker*

--Arleathia Chambliss Wright

Day Thirty-Four

Have you ever been in a situation where you had to make the decision to follow what God says to your heart because it was good, knowing if you did not, it would be bad for you?

Day Thirty-Five

Making Good Decisions

Read: Proverbs 16:33; 18:15 New International Version (NIV)

The lot is cast into the lap,
but its every decision is from the Lord.

The heart of the discerning acquires knowledge,
for the ears of the wise seek it out.

First, we ought to make sure we have all the facts before deciding. The bible says in Proverbs 18:15, "The heart of the discerning acquires knowledge, for the ears of the wise seek it out." A person who really wants to understand something will do his research. Once they acquire the knowledge, it creates new ideas.

We are always open to new ideas. We use those ideas to write books, open a business, and to help someone in need. Some may use those ideas to create bad habits causing harm to others. As our mind is open to new ideas, we must seek God's guidance. Do your research with His word. The idea will become much clearer to you. Some may decide to seek the advice of trusted friends. However, let's be clear that our decision is not based on values that contradicts God's word.

I contemplated a lot about moving to Florida. First, I thought, I cannot leave my siblings. Then, I did not want to leave my church, friends, and classmates. I knew I would miss going and doing for them all. People tell me all the time how wonderful my children are and since I am getting older, I should go live with my children in Florida. Some nights, I started having nightmares about my children when they were kids. I would pray to God asking him, “what are you trying to tell me?” I felt so loved being around them in the dream. They needed me and I needed them. I guess the good Lord was saying, it is ok Alma, I give you permission to go be with your children.

Advice from friends is okay, but make sure you seek Him first. Knowing what the word and the wisdom it gives, encourages our decision making and provides us with the discernment we need to make healthy choices. Using the principles of truth found in God’s word is consistent with the right decisions we make. There are so many choices and opinions we encounter before making decisions, it is hard to know which is the one from God. Proverbs 16:33 states “The lot is cast into the lap, but its every decision is from the LORD.” The outcome of our decisions is determined by the Lord our God. If only one of the ideas you have pleases God, then that is the right choice. If your ideas are consistent with God’s word, trust God to help you plan them so that you will be successful in the decisions you make that will Glorify Him.

Let us Pray:

Father God, help me in my decision making. Help me have the discernment to know that all decisions must come from you. I want to fulfill the purpose you have for me in the decisions I make. I know I have made some mistakes before, but I know you will forgive me and help me to make better decisions.
In Jesus name I pray. Amen

Song to Ponder: *I will Trust in the Lord – Baptist Hymn*

--Alma Jean Chambliss

Day Thirty-Five

Share a time when God helped you make a good decision.

Day Thirty-Six

Minister To Yourself

Read: Joshua 1:9 New International Version (NIV)

Have I not commanded you? Be strong and courageous. Do not be afraid; do not be discouraged, for the Lord your God will be with you wherever you go."

Have you ever felt so low about your circumstances that instead of seeking support from your loved ones, you had to motivate yourself? Thank the Lord I have learned how to do this. If you are like me, you may call your momma, your sister, or any other family members or friends, but still feel discouraged. The feelings about that situation caused doubts, fears, insecurities, hopelessness, and faithlessness. You even said a prayer, but it felt like God was not getting the message.

The first step is to pray about it, put it in His hand, and trust in Him. We deviate from the steps immediately after we pray. This is when we start calling around to see who has the encouraging words to give to us to help us get through the situation, or to help us snap out of the 'funk'. Well, we make the calls, and discover that they are going through the same thing, or something different. Or maybe they have never been in the situation and cannot give you the advice you need. So, you are back where you started.

The Lord said to Joshua to be strong and courageous. With much prayer and devotion, a songwriter said, speak over yourself and encourage yourself in the Lord. David, in 1 Samuel 30:6, encouraged himself in the Lord. We must learn how to encourage ourselves in the

Lord. In some situations, you will learn how to encourage yourself faster than at any other time. The bible says that God is our present help in the times of a storm. Sing praises, read the scriptures, trust the promises of the Lord, then speak a word over yourself. I will no longer be stressed. I will no longer be insecure. I will no longer feel hopeless. You must speak all these things during your test. Jesus said, if you have the faith of a mustard seed, you will be able to move mountains in Jesus' name.

Let us Pray:

Thank you, father, for my strength and courageousness not to be afraid and discouraged. I will encourage myself knowing that you are with me wherever I go.

Song to Ponder: *Encourage Yourself – Donald Lawrence & the Tri-City Singers*

--Arleathia Chambliss Wright

Day Thirty-Six

Have you ever felt so low about your circumstances that instead of seeking support from your loved ones, you had to motivate yourself?

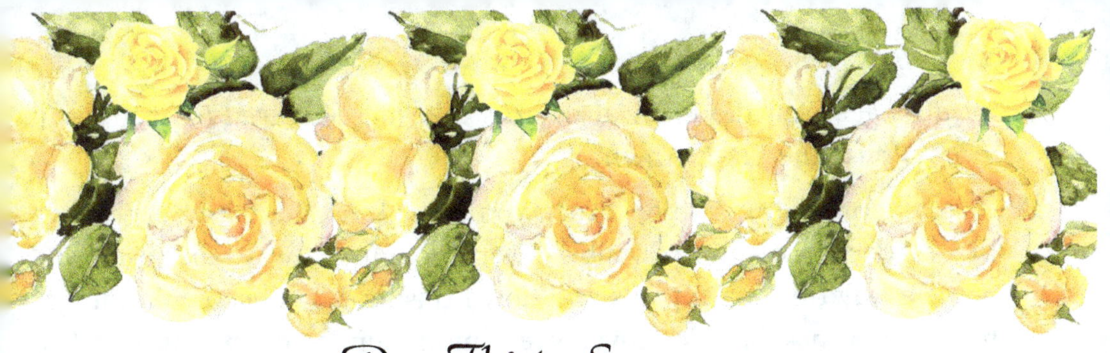

Day Thirty-Seven

Mountain Moving Faith

Read: Mark 11: 22 -24 New International Version (NIV)

22 "Have faith in God," Jesus answered. 23 "Truly[a] I tell you, if anyone says to this mountain, 'Go, throw yourself into the sea,' and does not doubt in their heart but believes that what they say will happen, it will be done for them. 24 Therefore I tell you, whatever you ask for in prayer, believe that you have received it, and it will be yours.

Faith in God is the only thing that will keep us going crazy when we are having a rough time. I know because I have been in a rough time. It all began when my daughter became handicap. I prayed and cried every day. At first, I was told that she would not live past 16 years old. I could not believe it. I begin to pray every day and all day. I prayed to get help for her. My prayers were answered. God knew I needed some help. There was a clinic for Cripple Children out of town. I knew if God answered the prayer, he would make a way for transportation to get there. I did not have to worry. I put my faith in God. Every time I had an appointment at the Cripple Children clinic, he made provisions for transportation.

I never had problems getting help for my daughter. No matter where we had to go or the plans we had for her, God took care of us no matter when or where. Thank you, Jesus! What an awesome God we serve. I would not have made it without Him. Because I put my faith in God, she lived longer than the medical doctors told me. She lived 53 wonderful years. Praise the Lord. Amen.

With something as big as this, you must keep the faith and believe that God can do the impossible. Even though she was handicap, God made a way through my ups and down raising a handicap child. It was hard sometimes, but He moved every mountain for me because I asked and trusted him to do so.

Let Us Pray:

Father God, thank you for all that you do for me. Thank you for giving me, Daphany. Thank you for giving me everything I asked for to help me with her. My faith never wavered during the rough times. I always believe in you and know you will continue to see me through. Bless those who put their faith in you Jesus. I am a living testimony of what You can do the impossible and continues to do so.
In Jesus name Amen.

Song to Ponder: *Never would have made it -- Warren Sapp*

--*Alma Jean Chambliss*

Day Thirty-Seven

Describe a time that it was necessary to use your mountain moving faith.

Day Thirty-Eight

Live For TODAY!!!

Read: Psalm 118:24 New International Version (NIV)

This is the day the Lord has made; We will rejoice and be glad in it.

This is the day the lord has made let us rejoice and be glad IN IT. As I have gotten older and going through my challenges of anxiety, worrisome, disappointments, and financial hardships, I have come to realize that God is in control. God is on the throne. God will fight these battles.

If you have woken up this morning, He made this day for you. You cannot control yesterday for it is already gone. You cannot do anything about tomorrow because you do not know what it is going to bring. So, guess what? Live for today!!

That is what this verse means to me. It is telling me to live for today because tomorrow is not promised. Live for today because you are alive and well. Live for today because you have ALL your senses. Live for today because you have a job. Live for today because you have a roof over your head and the mortgage is paid for the month. Live for today because the lights are on, and the car note is paid. Live for today because there is food in the cabinets and the refrigerator. Live for today because there are clothes on your back. You may have spoken to your family and friends, and they are well today.

What are you complaining for? This IS the day the Lord has made.

Let us rejoice and be glad IN IT!!! IN TODAY!! Hallelujah!

Let us Pray:

Thank you, father, for letting me see another day. Thank you for all that I have. Thank you that my bills are in order. Thank you that my family and friends are well.
I will rejoice and be glad.
In your precious name Amen!

Song to Ponder: *This is the Day -- Fred Hammond*

--Arleathia Chambliss Wright

Day Thirty-Eight

For what reason do you have to celebrate today?

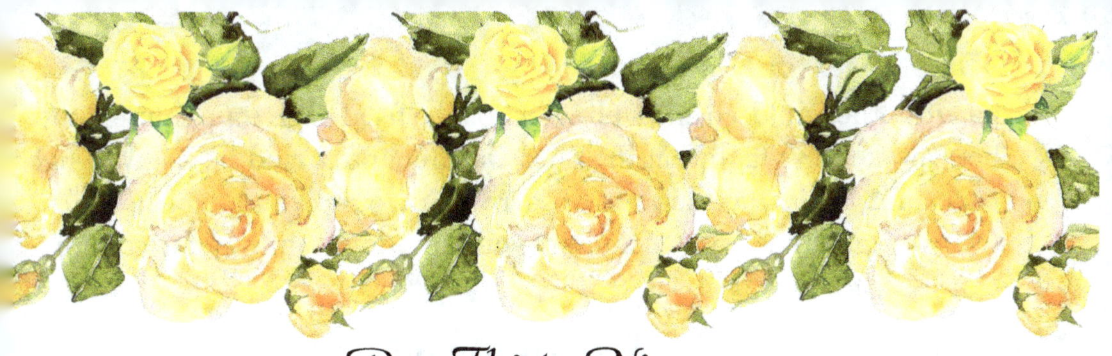

Day Thirty-Nine

Comfort From The Lord

Read: Matthew 5:4 New International Version (NIV)

Blessed are those who mourn, for they will be comforted.

God said that he would comfort us in the times of a storm. A storm could be the death of a loved one or adversities in life. If you believe in his promises, they will comfort you. Open the Bible and read what he has to say about his promises. We are blessed when we are mourning because we have the comforts of the Lord. You must study his word and believe that he is there for you during your time of sorrow. You must look to him for comfort. God is our Comforter. Do not let the enemy tell you otherwise. If you do not go to him for comfort, you may seek the wrong type of comfort. The wrong type of comfort may be foods, drugs, sex, or the wrong crowd. These types of comfort are temporary when God's comfort is everlasting. Hold to his hand, God unchanging hand.

I can remember when my children were little, I had a hard time comforting them before they went to bed. They did not want to go to bed when it was time to go. I would sing and read a bedtime story to them and have them to say their prayers. I did this to help comfort them. To let them know that God was watching over them and would protect and comfort them. They enjoyed it. I thanked God for helping me comfort them. They believed in their prayers enough which help comfort them to finally fall asleep.

We all will lose a loved one. God said he blesses those who mourn, and they will be comforted. I lost my husband and my daughter. God comforted me. He put people around me to help comfort me. I especially had my other children and siblings who God used to give me courage and help awaken my faith that the Lord was in control, and he knows what is best for us during the time of sorrow. Surround yourself with others who will pray for God to comfort you. You, too, can pray for comfort. God is just a prayer away.

Let us pray:

Father God, thank you for being the Comforter. When we are in uncomfortable situations, you show up and show out. We need you lord in every situation that causes us to feel uncomfortable. Help us to understand that you have all power to comfort and keep us. That we should never turn to anyone or anything but you. You are our resource. We pray this in your holy name,
Amen.

Song to Ponder: *Comforter – Cee Cee Winans*

--Alma Jean Chambliss

Day Thirty-Nine

Describe a time when you needed comfort from the Lord.

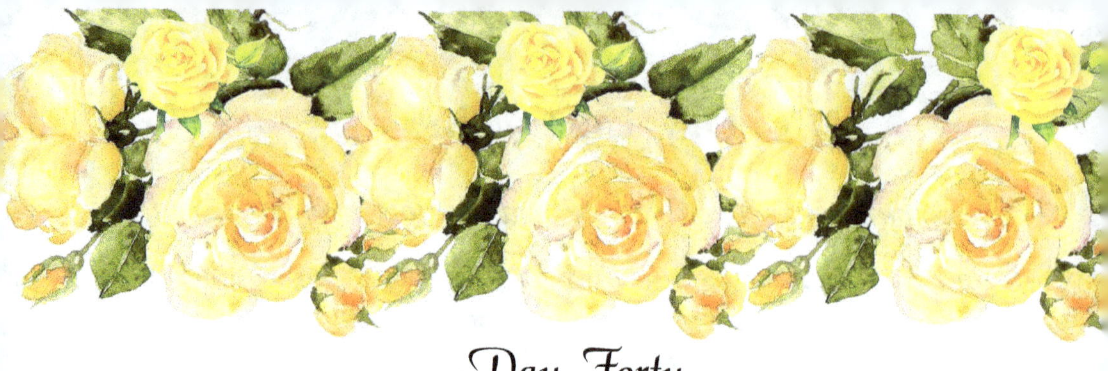

Day Forty

Seek First The Kingdom

Read: Matthew 6:33 New International Version (NIV)

33 But seek first his kingdom and his righteousness, and all these things will be given to you as well.

We often make plans before we ask God. That is when things go wrong. Have you asked, "God why do I keep failing. Where is my breakthrough? God said he would give me the desires of my heart, but when?" We look at how others get their blessings and think we can and will get ours the same way. It does not work that way.

For example, you decide to become an entrepreneur, and receive a few certifications and trades. Then ultimately quit your job. As you run your business, the first failure, and second failure happens. You begin to wonder why. You wonder why your family member, friend or associate have such successful businesses. There is a possibility that they got on their knees to pray to God for the success of their business. They may have asked for favor from the Lord to lead them and guide them in the right direction. They may have asked the Lord to enlarge their territory. Maybe they made Him a promise to give Him ALL the credit for their success and glorify Him for making the business possible and profitable. No, you did not see what went own behind closed doors with this individual. None of these matters! What God has for you, is for you.

You are only responsible for yourself in your relationship with God.

God said, I know the plans I have for you. Seek, first, the kingdom of God and His righteousness, and all these things shall be added to you. He said, ALL THINGS will be added to you. So, when you decided to start a business without the help of the Lord, your business failed.

Now go to God in prayer first. Make sure it is the plan that He has for you. Ask the Holy Spirit to help you. When the time is right for you to start your business, you will know for sure this time and it will prosper because He said so.

Let us Pray:

Dear Lord, teach us to come to you first seeking your righteousness so that all things will be added to us. In Jesus name Amen.

Song to Ponder: *Seek and Ye Shall Find*

--Arleathia Chambliss Wright

Day Forty

What are some plans you have made without first, seeking God?

Day Forty-One

Jesus Prayer

Read: John 17:1-2 New International Version (NIV)

17 After Jesus said this, he looked toward heaven and prayed: "Father, the hour has come. Glorify your Son, that your Son may glorify you. 2 For you granted him authority over all people that he might give eternal life to all those you have given him.

The time had come for Jesus to let His disciples know that he was leaving them to be with the Father. He kneeled and began to pray to His Father praying to be glorified. He also prayed for His disciples and all the believers. It brings me joy to read this prayer. Jesus loved being with His disciples and had a hard time leaving them behind. However, Jesus had done all there was to do on earth. With obedience, He brought glory to God here on earth. Jesus was given the authority over all His people offering us eternal life. God asked him to do these things you may have read about, and now it is time for God to glorify Him. He prayed for us to believe all that He had taught the disciples. Everything He revealed to them should help all of us.

I can imagine how Jesus went to the Father and prayed for us. I am sure He prayed, "Father God, the one who knows all, sees all, hears all, and owns all, please give all Your people strength to endure the trials and tribulations of this world. Please ensure they remember what I taught the disciples. Please help them to obey and carry out Your plans lovingly with good measure as I did. No matter what happens, do not allow their trials to break them. The world needs You right now. Let them know that You are everywhere. I gave them the words You gave Me. Your word is true. Protect them with My name, the name You gave Me. I sacrifice myself so they can be sanctified. Let thy message be heard to all who believe. Now that they know You, and that You sent Me, I am in them as You are in Me. Amen"

Let Us Pray:

Jesus, pray for me. Pray that God will sustain me through all my trials and tribulations. Pray that He gives me the wisdom and power He gave you. Pray that He would order my steps and lead me to my destiny that He has for me. Pray that now that I know you, I am sanctified. Glorify Him in the name of Jesus. Amen

Song to Ponder: *Say A Prayer ---Donald Lawrence & Faith Evans*

--Alma Jean Chambliss

Day Forty-One

Write a prayer that you think Jesus used to pray for us.

Day Forty-Two

Peace From The Throne

Read: Isaiah 26:3 New International Version (NIV)

You will keep in perfect peace
those whose minds are steadfast,
because they trust in you.

God said if you remember that He is on the throne and in control, you will find your peace. Often, we forget that God is on the throne. He is the Prince of Peace and Lord of Lord. He sees all and knows all. When you are in a funk over the disappointments, loss of a loved one, and financially stricken, remember peace comes from the throne.

There is so much going on in the world that we lose focus on knowing where our peace comes from. Hearing that your child is acting out in school, losing your job, losing a loved one, stressing over little things, trying to keep up with other people, watching the news, and juggling a lot of things can get in the way of the peace you deserve.

Often, I have been in this predicament where I would allow the world to take over my thoughts to the point, I lose control of who I am in Christ. In traffic, I may get angry and swear; Call a few people to gossip; on Sundays, I may stay in the bed; When I am anxious, I may cry and wonder why. I do this until the holy spirit recalls, who my father is and telling me to just trust Him. He will keep me in perfect peace.

Pray and ask God to drown out the noise so that you can hear Him so that He can give you His peace from the throne.

Let us Pray:

Lord, we ask you right now to drown out the noise of this world so we can hear your voice. We need a word from you to help us through our circumstances so that we can have the peace You give from the throne.
Amen

Song to Ponder: *Smokie Norful – I need a Word from You.*

--Arleathia Chambliss Wright

Day Forty-Two

What is going on in the world that you have lost focus on knowing where your peace comes from?

Day Forty-Three

The Bible Is Our Map

Read: Psalm 119:105-106 New International Version (NIV)

105 Your word is a lamp for my feet, a light on my path.
106 I have taken an oath and confirmed it, that I will follow your righteous laws.

Studying the word every day helps us to grow closer to God. In these verses, the Psalmist tells us to study God's love and meditate on it every day. God's word is a commandment, testimony, precepts and judgements. It is also sweeter than honey and a lamp unto our feet and a light to our path.

If you think about the Global Positioning System known as GPS, Google defines it as a utility provide users with positioning, navigation, and timing services. Someone thought of this brilliant idea to record the directions needed for us to navigate from place to place, especially the places we are not familiar with.

From a biblical perspective, someone also brilliantly recorded sacred writings in the bible. The bible is our map that provides the readers with positioning, navigation, and timing services as well. The scriptures walk us through the life before and after Christ describing His will, laws, nature, saving all humanity. We can use the bible as a vehicle for God to communicate with His people granting us spiritual directions in our lives. Those who believe in His word can navigate through different scripture readings according to their circumstances, finding answers needed to get them through. Studying the word can also position you to become saved and eventually a disciple of Christ where Jesus said in Matthew 28:19 to go and make disciples of all nations, baptizing them in the name of the Father and of the Son and of the Holy Spirit. The timing system sets up chronological events from different books of the bible that describes what happened before and after Christ. We can use the events from each book as an opportunity to know and build a relationship with God.

Use the bible as a road map for reading, studying, and meditating on the word of God to help you to grow in the Lord and Savior Jesus Christ. This should be a constant guide to help us find our way and stay on course. We must seek him with an open heart and willing spirit.

Let us Pray:

Lord, guide us from above with your continuous
love as we trust you to lead us and guide us in the right
direction. When we go in the wrong direction,
please lead us back to you. Now father, we know that if we
follow Your word every day, we will be headed in
the right direction.
In Jesus name we pray, Amen.

Song to Ponder: *Guide Me O Thou Great Jehovah*

--Alma Jean Chambliss

Day Forty-Three

Describe a time when God's word was a lamp unto your feet.

Day Forty-Four

A Heart Fully Committed

Read: 2 Chronicles 16:9 New International Version (NIV)

"...The eyes of the LORD search the whole earth in order to strengthen those whose hearts are fully committed to him..."

The race is not given to the swift or to the strong. Jesus chose His disciples who did not have it all together. He could have chosen the Pharisees who played by the religious rules and did all that they thought was right, but their hearts were not right. Jesus selected a few good men who had imperfections and no religious upbringing. We call ourselves Christians, but we fail when it comes to judging people. Christians look at how people look, what they have, their background and their status.

Good news!!! God sees beyond all that. I can testify to this. When I keep my eyes on Him, He sees my heart. He knows the future. He chooses the ones who are committed to Him. He knows the purpose He will fulfill in your life. He is not looking for perfection. He is looking for people who seek Him and know that He is where the help comes from. Scripture says, in 2 Chronicles 16:9, "The eyes of the LORD search the whole earth in order to strengthen those whose hearts are fully committed to him." He knows your heart to know that your actions that are not perfect need improvement, but he is delighted in those who are delighted in Him. He will show up strong in your life. He will show the unimaginable if you would fully commit your heart to Him.

Let us Pray:

Father God, I want to be fully committed to You. Please clean my heart of the things that are not pleasing to you so my heart.
In Jesus name, Amen.

Song to Ponder: *Fully Committed.*

--Arleathia Chambliss Wright

Day Forty-Four

In what way is your heart fully committed to God? If no way, how will you change your heart?

Day Forty-Five

Being Afraid In The Dark

Read: Deuteronomy 4:31 New International Version (NIV)

31 For the Lord your God is a merciful God; he will not abandon or destroy you or forget the covenant with your ancestors, which he confirmed to them by oath.

God is merciful and will not abandon us. He is always there. Just ask Him for what you need. He will be there if you believe. You must believe that he is there when you call on Him.

When I was a little girl, I was afraid of the dark growing up. After getting use to the dark at one house, when we moved from one house to another, the fear would start again. There was a street light at one of the houses we lived that would shine bright through the window into my room. When we moved again, I was afraid to walk alone in the dark, but when my father walked beside me and took my hand, all my fears went away. I trusted my father to lead and guide me through the darkness. I trusted him because he loved me and would not let anything happen to me.

This works in any situation where you feel you are in a dark place. You must trust in our heavenly Father. When you feel afraid, grab His hands and He will see you through. Get to know him so that you can trust him to lead you and guide you out of the fears and circumstances preventing you from moving forward. Your safety is in His hands. God loves you and will not let anything happen to you. Now, when I go to bed at night, I pray that God, my father in heaven will take care of me in the dark. He is merciful and will not abandon me.

Let us Pray:

Heavenly Father, please continue to take care of me. Remove the fears that plague my mind and drive me to despair. I trust you and know that you will never leave me or forsake me.
In Jesus name I pray. Amen

Song to Ponder: *Great is your mercy – Donnie McClurkin*

--Alma Jean Chambliss

Day Forty-Five

Describe a time you were in the dark, a dark part of you life. Who was there for you and help bring you out?

Day Forty-Six

Credited Righteousness

Read: Romans 4:20–24 New International Version

20 Yet he did not waver through unbelief regarding the promise of God but was strengthened in his faith and gave glory to God, 21 being fully persuaded that God had power to do what he had promised. 22 This is why "it was credited to him as righteousness." 23 The words "it was credited to him" were written not for him alone, 24 but also for us, to whom God will credit righteousness—for us who believe in him who raised Jesus our Lord from the dead.

Have there ever been a time you did not waver through unbelief regarding a promise God made to you? I have seen his promise fulfilled time and time again because I believe and trust in Him who raised Christ Jesus from the grave. After high school, I left home for the first time, God promised to take care of me; and He did. I was pregnant with child in college and had no clue how to raise a baby, God promised to provide a way giving me, Motherly Instincts. I raised a child alone while attending school; His promise was sufficient. Once I learned to surrender all to Him and leave it with Him, this strengthened my faith. Glory to God.

Did you know that because you are a child of God, you are accepted and approved through your faith in Him the same way He accepted

Abraham in Romans 4:23-24? He credits all righteousness for those who believe in Him. As he did for Abraham, He will do it for us. I give Him all the credit, all the glory, and all the honor for all that He does for me.

Trust and believe with all righteousness, and He will strengthen you.

Let us Pray:

Thank you, Lord for being the Lord of Abraham and my God too. Thanks for accepting and approving of me because of my faith in You. I am thankful for who I am and who created me. I will continue to lean on Your promises giving you all the glory and all the praises.
In Jesus name I pray.

Song to Ponder: *Leaning on the promises of God. --Baptist Hymn*

--Arleathia Chambliss Wright

Day Forty-Six

Describe a time you did not waver through unbelief regarding a promise God made to you.

Day Forty-Seven

Breaking The Habit

Read: James 5:16 New International Version (NIV)

16 Therefore confess your sins to each other and pray for each other so that you may be healed. The prayer of a righteous person is powerful and effective.

Our sinful nature is a habit none of us can break completely, but a pattern of sinful living shows that we may not be serious about following God. Some habits we may be able to break, and some habits that may be accidental. These bad habits cause us to sin.

Some of us do not want anyone to see our bad habits. People have struggles with addictions and bad habits they are embarrassed about. Habits such as drug addictions, depressions, and homosexuality. We are not perfect. God still loves us. If you are still having problems in an area of bad habits, get some help. Seek God first and he will direct your path to the help you need. Then, the scripture tells us to admit the habit to someone and pray for each other that you may be healed. Be honest with yourself. The person you confide in should be someone you trust, someone who will stand in faith with you, and most of all, someone who will pray for you.

We never know what people are going through unless they talk about it. You may be surprised. The experience of someone else may possibly be like yours. I am sure there are millions of stories just like yours. Do not let the shame isolate you. Healing is in honesty. Chains cannot be broken on your own. The fear of what others will think, will block you from breaking the habit. Call on the Lord and trust Him first.

Let's break every chain today.

Let us Pray:

Father God. We are praying for each other for strength to fight any addictions or bad habits we encounter. We admit our faults, Lord. We just want to get through this sinful living and have a better life following you. You are a healer. Help us be and advocate for someone else while glorifying You. Please touch right now in the name of Jesus. Amen.

Song to Ponder: *Break Every Chain – Tasha Cobbs Leonard*

--Alma Jean Chambliss

Day Forty-Seven

With the Lord's help, describe a sinful habit that was too hard for you to break and what you had to do to break it.

Day Forty-Eight

There Are Better Things In Store

Read: Ruth 2: 8-9 New International Version (NIV)

8 So Boaz said to Ruth, "My daughter, listen to me.
Don't go and glean in another field and don't go away
from here. Stay here with the women who
work for me. 9 Watch the field where the men are
harvesting and follow along after the women.

You never know who is watching. There are people watching you during your ups and downs. Someone may be waiting for the right time to help you by sharing resources they have. They may want to see you do better. Have you ever been on a job only to make ends meet? You may have mixed feelings about this type of move, but your faith tells you, it is going to get better. There are better days coming. Reminding yourself that you were working there just until you land your career job.

I have been in this situation. I was working with this guy for a few weeks who asked, "why are you working in a place like this with a degree." I told him this position was to help pay bills. Not to say I could not handle it, but it was rough hours and hard dirty work. This was something I had not done since college, but I did it. As it turns out, he knew the manager of the IT company of a major telecommunications company who he reached out to about me. I sent my resume, interviewed, and was hired. God had better things in store for me after that situation.

Remember the story of Ruth, how she decided to be kind and care for her mother-in-law, Naomi? She left her family to be with her mother-in-law after the death of her husband and sons. When Ruth and Naomi started to run out of food, Ruth went to the fields to pick up the leftover barley that was dropped by the harvesters. She planned take the barley back home to help feed them both. As she continued to do this, Ruth did not know Boaz, the wealthy man who own the fields, was watching her. He would ask the workers to drop more barley intentionally for her. Ruth saw the blessing of the Lord who was providing a way for food for her and her mother-in-law. She was grateful. What she did not see, there was something better in store for her. Boaz begin to find out more about Ruth and fell in love with her and married her. Now, instead of working in the field, she ended up owning the field.

Just like Ruth, God will surprise you and have better things in store for you. Hold on to your seats, God is not done. He will surprise you and give you more than you could ever ask for. He knows what you have been through and what you are going through. There are better things in store for you. Please be prepared for blessings unimaginable.

Let us Pray:

Father God, thank you for blessing me, repeatedly. I choose to believe today that there are better things in store for me, because you are God and you said so. I declare and decree that everything is working for my good. In Jesus name Amen.

Song to Ponder: *Better – Hezekiah Walker or Better Days are coming – Le'Andria Johnson*

--Arleathia Chambliss Wright

Day Forty-Eight

What were the better things God has provided for you?

Day Forty-Nine

Study The Bible For Yourself

Read: 2 Timothy 2:15 King James Version (KJV)

"Study to shew thyself approved unto God, a workman that needeth not to be ashamed, rightly dividing the word of truth."

There are many guidelines' people have created to help you study of the Bible. The bottom line is that you have to make a commitment to set aside time to read and study the Bible. If you do not set aside that time, you will neglect it. Imagine it as an appointment with the Lord to have some quite time. I chose to begin to study in the mornings when I first awake. I was afraid that if I did not start in the morning, other things would get in the way and I would never get to the reading.

The first thing I do is thank God for waking me up to see another day. Then, I would pray and ask God to help me understand what I was about to read. Take your time and read carefully. The Holy Spirit will come into your mind and heart and help you to understand what you are reading. Sometimes you have to read slowly or over and over again to get the true meaning of the verses. Think about what the words may be saying to you. Do not get discourage, the Holy Spirit will help you. Let the spirit take control and guide you.

You should read and study the word for yourself. There are false teachers around us. Paul instructs Timothy to inform God's people that they must stop listening to these false teachers who would ruin their interpretation of God's word. There are some people who learn scripture and recite it so much that when you hear it, you try repeating without understanding what it means. You would not want to go on the words of what someone else saids about what is written in the word. The Bible says in 2 Timothy 2:15 to "study to show thyself approved unto God..." You want to study the God's word for yourself and allow the holy spirit to give you the true meaning. Make a commitment to study for yourself so you will know the truth. Knowing the truth will set you free.

Let us Pray:

Dear Lord, thank you that your Word is true.
Thank you for the Holy Spirit who helps me to
understand your word as I read and meditate on it.
Giving you all the Glory and praise. Amen

--Alma Jean Chambliss

Day Forty-Nine

Describe a what God said to you and you said to Him when you studied the Bible for yourself.

Day Fifty

My Sinful Nature

Read: Col. 3: 1-7 & Romans 7:14-24 New International Version (NIV)

So then, I myself in my mind am a slave to God's law, but in my sinful nature[b] a slave to the law of sin.

Are you tired of doing or thinking the same things as making bad decisions or choices and getting the same results? If so, do something different about this habitual act. Certainly, in my sinful nature, I have made and continue to make those bad decisions or choices as well. Some of the bad choices may include abusive relationship partners, being greedy, going to unwarranted events, smoking or drinking harmful substances, and hanging with evil people. I choose not to seek Him most of the time and make the decision myself. Even though I have learned that without seeking God first before making these decisions, the decision I make will fail every time. Is this you? Colossians 3:1-7 tells us to set our hearts and minds on things above where Christ is and not on earthly things. So, pray for strength to put away those sinful things you once lived because the wrath of the Lord is coming.

Guess what? Paul went through the same situation of making the wrong decisions. He felt trapped in his sinful nature not wanting to do God's will. I love the way he describes it in Romans 7:14-24. He said although he wants to do the right thing, his mind tells him to do otherwise. Can you relate? It is like a child being told not to touch a hot stove, but they touch it anyway. The results are hurtful. He went on to say that the sinful nature that lives within is not good. As Paul, we all have the desire to do what is right, but we do not follow through. We keep on doing the wrong. When we keep doing the wrong when we know it is not right, it is considered the sin that is in us that makes us do the wrong. This is us as a slave to sin.

However, in Romans 7:25, Paul found the answer to our dilemma to help us rescue us from being a slave to sin. Through Jesus Christ our Lord was an easy answer that you should appreciate. His law, the law of the Spirit sets us free from the law of sin and death. Amen. Hallelujah!

So now that we know the difference, thanks be to God who knows our hearts and renews our mind. He will deliver us from these bad decisions or choices. If we keep our mind focused on Him by saying to ourselves, "I am a slave to His law, but in my sinful nature, I am a slave to the law of sin. I will focus on Him and seek Him first before making bad decisions so that I will not become a slave to sin any longer. In Jesus name. Amen."

Let us Pray:

Lord, I am tired of my sinful ways. I want to set my heart and mind on you. Please take this cup from me so I can honor you. Thank you that I can come to you first before making any decisions. Please give me strength to endure this challenge.
In Jesus name.

Song to Ponder: *Wanna be Happy? – Kirk Franklin*

--Arleathia Chambliss Wright

Day Fifty

If you are making bad decisions or choices and getting the same results, what are you doing different about this habitual act?

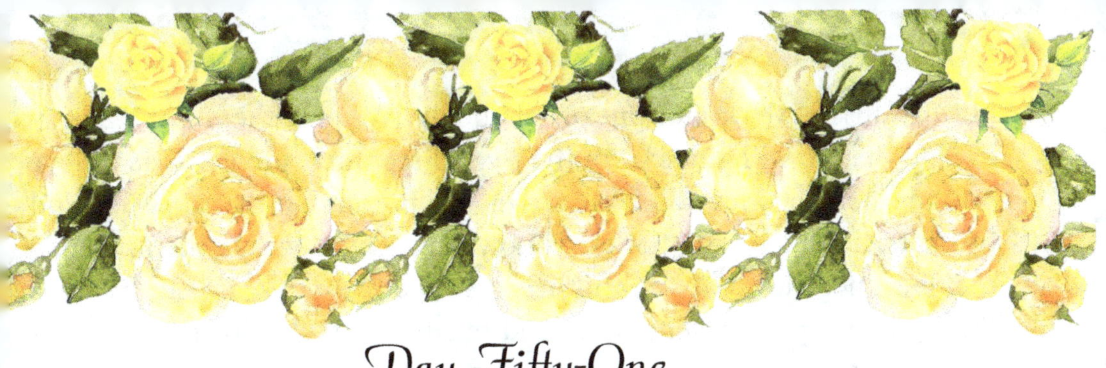

Day Fifty-One

Rooted In Love

Read: Hebrews 13:15-16 New International Version (NIV)

15 Through Jesus, therefore, let us continually offer to God a sacrifice of praise—the fruit of lips that openly profess his name. 16 And do not forget to do good and to share with others, for with such sacrifices God is pleased.

Let the roots of God's love in our life be entwined with others who need our support with Jesus help let us continue to offer sacrifices and praise to God by glorifying his name. Let us not forget to share what we must for those that are in need. For this is pleasing to God.

Look at Family. The Meaning of a family to me is showing the same love God has shown and being loved by family members in the same manner regardless of their success and failures. The foundation must be strong, and Jesus must be in the mist. Everything must be in order. Christ first, the husband, the wife and then the children. The family represents the image of Christ on Earth. Christ is the main key element of the family. When Christ is in the midst, then there is love overflowing.

In my family, God is the head. Prayer is the first thing I do in the morning. If I miss my prayer, my day does not go right for me. All during the day, I am thanking Jesus. My children were taught about the love of God and how to pray. This helps us to love everybody as if they are one of the family. We should not treat people different because they are not in Christ. We do not put people down. We pick them up. We pray to God that he will guide us in the right direction leading others to love one another as he loved us. We are to stay in touch with our sisters and brothers, because we do not ever know when we may need them. Family members need love for one another. We need them to share our burdens through a support system. This kind of support will help strengthen us which activates love in many areas of our life. God's love is rooted deep down in our soul. If you and your family know anything about God's love, be encouraged and come together showing love and praying for one another. That's what rooted in love is all about. Whatever is going on in our lives, the answer is always love.

Let us Pray:

Thank you, heavenly father for giving us your love that is deeply rooted in us. Help us to tap into your love so that we can love others the same. Family means everything to me and because you are rooted in us, our love will overflow for one another.
In Jesus name. Amen.

Song to Ponder: *Jesus loves me this I know – Old Spiritual Hymn*

--Alma Jean Chambliss

Day Fifty-One

Describe times you have shown love with the fruit of your lips and actions that are pleasing to God.

Day Fifty-Two

Humility Towards One Another

Read: 1 Peter 5:5-8 New International Version (NIV)

5 In the same way, you who are younger, submit yourselves to your elders. All of you, clothe yourselves with humility toward one another, because,
"God opposes the proud
but shows favor to the humble."[a]

With all that is going on in this world, we need to be the most obedient to His word. God has blessed us all to be here in the times of many storms. You may be going through a divorce, an addiction challenge, the loss of a loved one and the loss of a job, but God is still on the throne. He would like us to be uplifting to those who are going through some storms. During this time, humility towards one another is crucial, essential, and most of all, it is the key to help uplift one another. We never know what people are going through during their storms. Storms affect the mental and physical aspects of your body that can become deadly if you do not get the help and if you do not have the support you need. The challenges of life are not easy. So let us humble ourselves.

The bible says in 1 Peter 5:5, God opposes the proud, but shows favor to the humble. So do not be so proud when you are going through storms. If you need to start over and regroup, humble yourself and do what you need to do until God shows you favor. Do not consider your situation as a failure. We are all human and we all have had storms that we have gone through or going through right now. It is time to humble yourselves so that God may lift you up in His time. Watch your back. The enemy is busy planning his way to the proud one. The enemy can use the proud one to break up marriages, encourage addictions and frustrate the jobless.

So now that you know that we all go through these storms, show someone some love today by having humility towards one another. Stretch out your hand, lift a finger, and be a voice. One day, this might be you.

Let Us Pray:

Father God, teach me to humble myself in the times of a storm. Not only that, teach me to humble myself when I know that there are others in a storm. Teach me to want to help them in their time of need knowing that where they are in the challenges of life, I once was or will be. We all need one another, and you said we must love one another, and you show favor to the humble. I humble myself to you today, Lord. In Jesus name I pray. Amen

Song to Ponder: *Give me you – Shana Wilson*

--Arleathia Chambliss Wright

Day Fifty-Two

Name a time you have shared humility towards someone? How did you do it?

Day Fifty-Three

The Bread Of Life

Read: John 6:27 New International Version (NIV)

27 Do not work for food that spoils, but for food that endures eternal life, which the Son of Man will give you. For on him God the Father has placed his seal of approval."

So even though Jesus performed the miracle feeding 5000 people with 5 loaves of bread and two little fish, the people still did not believe in the Son of God. They had seen it with their own eyes and still did not believe in him. We all know people like that. They came to Jesus looking for more food. The people did not realize that Jesus is the Bread of Life. The type of bread we are looking for does not keep us full. Plus, the type of drink we consume makes us thirst for more. Jesus told them that they were looking for the wrong thing. They need to be looking for spiritual food and drink that gives them everlasting life.

Once they asked Jesus to give them this food and drink that last forevermore, Jesus explained, "I am the bread of life. He that cometh to me will hunger no more and he that believeth in me will thirst no more."

Some of us do not understand and believe how real this is. When we go to Jesus and ask Him for something, it's usually something that takes a miracle that only God can do. This should give you the everlasting life he gives us. Never having to go to anyone else but him. He will supply

ALL our needs to where we want to cry, hunger or thirst no more.

Jesus is the bread of life. God sent Jesus so we would hunger or thirst no more. Spiritual bread, the Word of God, gives us everlasting life like eating physical bread gives us physical life. Remember the Lord's prayer, 'Give us this day our daily bread'. Our daily bread comes from the one who was sent by God. We need His guidance and wisdom every day. As the songwriter sings, "Bread of Heaven, feed me so I want no more. Fill my cup, fill it up, and make me whole."

Let us Pray:

Bread of Heaven, give us this day our daily bread.
Please feed me until I want no more. Fill my cup, Lord.
Fill it up and make me whole.

Songs to Ponder: *Fill my Cup Lord by Cee Cee Winans*

--Alma Jean Chambliss

Day Fifty-Three

Describe when you realized the Bread of Life was real and what did you do to embrace it.

Day Fifty-Four

Jesus Will Carry You Through

Read: Isaiah 41:10 New International Version (NIV)

So do not fear, for I am with you;
do not be dismayed, for I am your God.
I will strengthen you and help you;
I will uphold you with my righteous right hand.

There are a lot of people going through some things right now. Loved ones are dying from not only the ailments high blood pressure, high cholesterol, diseases, car accidents and overdoses, but the plague that has hit this world, called Covid-19. I am here to tell you that God has been with us and carried us through storms like this before, and he will do it again.

God called Isaiah to become His servant to help with the Israelites in their times of storm. In Isaiah 41:10, God said to Isaiah, "do not fear, for I am with you; do not be dismayed, for I am your God." During the times of hardship, crisis, and sorrow, God is with us. He is our Comforter. Like he told Isaiah, do not be afraid, I am with you. Know that the same message is intended for us. We are not alone. During your crisis, recite those words, I am not alone, God is with me. It is easier said than done, but we must practice it, then believe it. David knew he was not alone in Psalm 23:4 when he said, "Yea, though I walk through the valley of the shadow of death, I will fear no evil" because he believed that God was with him. Jesus even promised that 'lo, I am with you always, even until the end of the age.

God is with us even when our family and friends are not. Remember that God will take care of you during all your storms. As the songwriter said, "Jesus will carry you through. Ask the savior to help you, comfort, strengthen and keep you. He is willing to aid you. He will carry you through."

Let us Pray:

Father, we come to you today, asking for your help. Comfort, strengthen and keep us through these times we are going through. We will no longer be afraid because we are not alone. We know that you are with us and will continue to carry us through. Thank you for being God and upholding us with your righteous right hand.
In Jesus name. Amen

Song to Ponder: *Hymn: Jesus will carry you through*

--Arleathia Chambliss Wright

Day Fifty-Four

Explain a time God carried you?

Day Fifty-Five

Life Through The Spirit

Read: Romans 8:13 New International Version (NIV)

13 For if you live according to the flesh, you will die; but if by the Spirit you put to death the misdeeds of the body, you will live.

We who are in Christ Jesus have life because Jesus set us free from condemnation. We are free from sin and death. God sent his son Jesus to do the unthinkable. He came in human form as a sin offering. Jesus condemned sin in flesh so that the Lord's righteousness and purpose would be fulfilled according to the spirit and not bound by the flesh.

See, those who are bound by flesh have no desire to honor God but have their minds set on fleshly desires. And those who live according to the spirit have their minds set on what the spirit desires.

Did you know we have life through the spirit? When you gave your life to Christ, you became a new creation. But the flesh, even though it's passed away, can get back up. Romans 8:13 says, "If you live by the flesh, you will die." It means that if you're always saying and doing what you feel like, your dreams and potential and relationships will die. It goes on to say, "But if through the Spirit, you mortify the flesh, you will live." To "mortify" means to keep it dead. You must decide to say no to the flesh.

As you read this scripture, agree that we have an obligation. So, follow the direction of the spirit and not the direction of the flesh. If you do not have the spirit within you, you do not belong to God nor do you have

His righteousness. He will give life in your mortal bodies through Jesus' spirit that dwells in you. The same way God gave Jesus' life as He raised him from the dead. So, what the law could not do, God was able to do by sending His son Jesus in the flesh so that his righteousness would be fulfilled. If the spirit is in you, God's purpose will be fulfilled no matter which path you take. He's always there.

Before I was saved, I used to say what was on my mind that really could hurt a person's feelings. But now that I am saved and filled with the spirit, I have learned to be more conscientious about what to say and when to say it or even how to speak my mind that would be gentle to the person's feelings.

Crucify the flesh. Be conscientious of what you are thinking before you do something that causes you to react to the flesh and not the spirit.

Let us Pray:

Thank you, Father, for always being there and giving me life in the spirit. I stray away sometimes, but I'm glad that when I dig deep within, I find your spirit that dwells in me. In Jesus name I pray. Amen

Song to ponder: *He's always there – CeeCee Winans*

--Alma Jean Chambliss

Day Fifty-Five

Describe a occasion where you chose to react in the spirit instead of the flesh.

Day Fifty-Six

God Comes Where You Are

Read: Psalms 113: 5-6 New International Version (NIV)

Who is like the Lord our God,
the One who sits enthroned on high,
6 who stoops down to look
on the heavens and the earth?

Have you ever thought that you were so low that God could not reach you? I have thought that a few times in my life. Well, there is good news that I am willing to share. When you are feeling low and nowhere to go, God will come where you are because all our help comes from Him.

If you are that person who is homeless, God will come into the homeless shelter. If you are that person who is always finding yourself in the drug house, God will come into the drug house. If you are that person who has been sentenced to prison, God will come into the prison. If you are that person who is so depressed and in your darkest place, God will come into that dark place. All you have to do is invite Him in.

We think that when we finally find a place to live, stop doing drugs, stop committing crimes, release from prison, and no longer suffer from depression, God will come to us and show us favor. This is not how God works. He comes to you in the middle of all your trials and tribulations. We all give in to some sort of temptation and the enemy comes to mind telling us we are done, you will never get better, your life is over, God is not going to help you. The God we serve is not like that. He is by your side.

God will come where you are no matter where you are in your storms including when you are down in the valley. Remember, he sits high and looks low. He sees everything. When you cannot see yourself coming up to His level, He said he will come to your level. God is all powerful and the creator of you. Do not be intimidated. God will come down and get dirty with you. He said in Jeremiah 29:11, "For I know the plans I have for you," declares the Lord, "plans to prosper you and not to harm you, plans to give you hope and a future." He has chosen you to fulfill His purpose.

Remember, when Jesus went into the hot furnace to get the Hebrew boys. He also went into the hog pen for the prodigal son. All this because, He comes to lift you from the dark place with no judgement. He comes to set you on a new path setting you free and forgiving you. Oh, what an awesome God we serve, Amen.

Let us Pray:

Thank you, God, for coming down to where I am. For finding me and uplifting me. For forgiving me and honoring me. I am glad that you came down to help me during the storms and while I was down in the valleys.
In my darkest hour, you have been my light.
What an awesome God we serve,
Amen.

Song to Ponder: *All of my help – Ricky Dillard*

--Arleathia Chambliss Wright

Day Fifty-Six

Name a time(s) you have thought that you were so low that God could not reach you?

Day Fifty-Seven

The Potter & The Clay

Read: Isaiah 64:8 New International Version (NIV)

Yet you, Lord, are our Father.
We are the clay, you are the potter;
we are all the work of your hand.

The Father, who art in heaven, wants to put you back together again. Did you know that our Father in Heaven is the Potter, and we are the clay? He has us in the palm of his hands. Therefore, He can shape us and mold us into anyone He wants us to be if you would allow Him.

At this time, you may be going through some things that keep you from allowing God to shape and mold you. You may think you are not pretty enough, smart enough, or maybe you are addicted to someone or something. You keep doing the same things and getting the same results. You have prayed for these obstacles to be removed from your presence and nothing has happened. You are waiting for God to answer.

I remember when I was a young teenager. I would help my mother raise her children. I remember saying to myself that when I get married and have kids, I want God to bless me to be the best mother for my children. He did just that. He made me love and care for them even when there were times I did not know how. As a result, my kids have grown to be blessed and loving as they were taught.

I am begging you to please trust the process. You do not have to remain in the shape that you are in. God is in control. He is behind the scenes working on your behalf. He is in the Potter's house. You are the clay on the Potter's wheel. You are next in line. Everything you need is in the Potter's house.

Let us Pray:

Thank you, Lord, for being the Potter and making me the clay. Mode me and make me into who you want me to be Lord. Not my will Lord but let thy will be done. In Jesus name. Amen

Song to Ponder: *VaShawn Mitchell - "The Potter's House"*

--Alma Jean Chambliss

Day Fifty-Seven

Describe a time when God removed some things in your life and put you back together.

Day Fifty-Eight

God's Divine Help

Read: Psalms 121: 1-2 New King James Version (NKJV)

I will lift up my eyes to the hills—
From whence comes my help?
2 My help comes from the Lord,
Who made heaven and earth.

Look to the hills which cometh your help. Your help comes from the Lord. He will send breakthroughs and create miracles to bring you out. Call upon him in the name of Jesus and be blessed. Know that God's divine help is on the way. Keep the faith that it is in His will and in His time. Your victory, deliverance, and breakthrough will come.

When I am going through trials and tribulations, I have learned that there is no other way but to seek Him lifting my eyes to the hills to which my help comes from. I have been depressed and discouraged. When I was out of work for a long period of time, I pulled out all my resources never thinking to slow down to seek God first. I kept hitting a brick wall. I was going down the wrong path not accomplishing anything to help myself. I was discouraged when the companies chose someone else. I was desperate because the bills were due. However, I was not desperate enough because I did not seek God first.

But God! When the light bulb came on in my head, I remembered Psalms 121: 1-2. God helps during our time of distress. He helps when we are depressed, confused, and ashamed. Has he ever opened doors for you that you did not think you could walk through? You may have gotten promotions that you did not think you were ready for; spoken to a crowd of people that you did not think you would be able to speak to; run a race you thought you would not finish. God's divine help, brought you through. That is who he is. Do as the scripture said and lift your eyes to where your help comes from.

Let us Pray:

Father God, thank you for your divine help. Thank you that when I look to you, I know that my help is coming. In Jesus name I pray, Amen.

Song to Ponder: *Jesus is my help – Hezekiah Walker*

--Arleathia Chambliss Wright

Day Fifty-Eight

What doors has God opened for you that you did not think you could walk through?

Day Fifty-Nine

The Living Water

Read: John 4:13-14 New King James Version (NKJV)

*13 Jesus answered and said to her, "Whoever drinks
of this water will thirst again, 14 but whoever
drinks of the water that I shall give him will
never thirst. But the water that
I shall give him will become in him a fountain
of water springing up into everlasting life."*

On Jesus' journey from Judea, he began to feel tired and sat down near this well, Jacob's well. He met a Samaritan woman at the well who comes to the well each day to draw water. As she and Jesus began to talk, Jesus gave her a message. The message was about the living water. Living water is a gift from God. Whoever drinks this water will not thirst again. This water is extraordinary, fresh, and pure that would satisfy your spiritual thirst forever more. This gift can only be given from Jesus Christ. It satisfies the soul's desires of many.

Have you ever been hungry and thirsty, but then ate and drank the thing you thought would satisfy the hunger and thirst you were feeling, but it didn't? You will hunger and thirst again. The physical function of our bodies hunger and thirst for food and water. If we go without eating or drinking for a long period of time, our bodies would be in a state of shock. We may get sick or cause other things to stop functioning. We would lose the energy the body needs to sustain itself. It is essential that we eat food and drink water.

Our spiritual functions, which is our soul, need spiritual food from the living Word which is Jesus Christ, and the written Word in the Bible to satisfy our hungry and thirsty soul. Living water is eternal life. You will hunger and thirst no more. The symbol of salvation given by God which gives us true knowledge of Jesus and the Holy Spirit who is always with us.

As Christians, we must share this living water with others so that God will shower down on them, and they will not thirst no more.

Let us Pray:

Lord, we thirst for you. We need you lord.
We need you in the land of the living. We need you to
shower down on us. Cleanse our souls. You know what we
stand in the need of. We thirst for you.
Open our hearts that we may receive your living
water and living word and never thirst again.
In Jesus' precious name. Amen

Song to Ponder: *Thirst for You – CeCe Winans*

--Alma Jean Chambliss

Day Fifty-Nine

Describe a time you experienced a great hunger and thirst for the Lord.

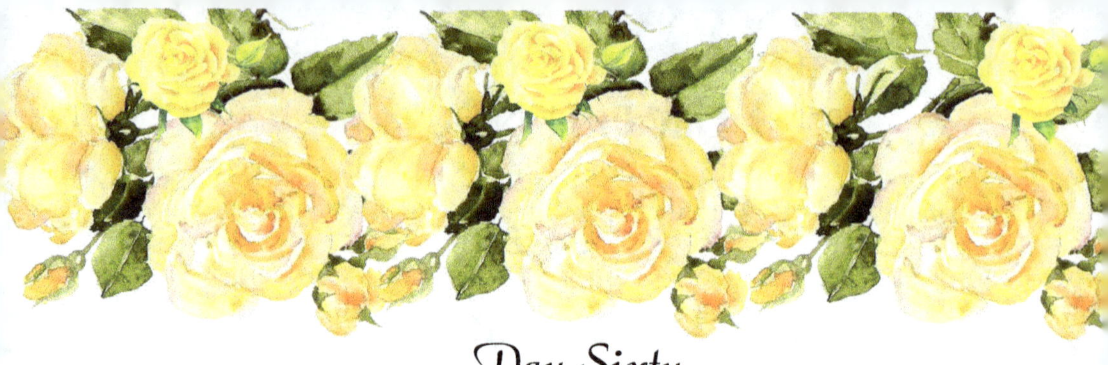

Day Sixty

Subject To Change

Read: Psalm 30:4-5 New International Version (NIV)

For His anger is but for a moment,
His favor is for life;
Weeping may endure for a night,
But [b]joy comes in the morning.

Do not get comfortable where you are, it is subject to change. Have you ever needed a quote for a vacation and the agent tells you, if you do not reserve the trip now, the price is subject to change? Our life lessons are like that when we go through some hardships or difficulties. Remember that trouble don't last always. The trouble is subject to change. In Psalm 30:4-5, David said, "Sing the praises of the Lord. His anger only lasts for a moment, but His favor lasts a lifetime. Weeping may endure for a night, but joy comes in the morning."

The hardship may consist of someone losing a job. But God! This situation is subject to change to them acquiring a better job with more money. You may be suffering from an illness that has plagued your life for years, but you have never given up. But God! This situation is subject to change where you are cured from this lifelong illness. Or you are in a car accident. Your legs are penned under the car and told you will never walk again. But God! This situation is subject to change where it is a miracle you can walk again. The judge gave you 30 years in prison. But God! This situation is subject to change to where you only do some or no years. Count it all joy in the Lord because joy comes in the morning.

Let us Pray:

Dear Heavenly Father. Thank you for teaching me that my troubles don't last always. That you are only angry for a moment, but your favor lasts a lifetime. I am excited and sing praises to you knowing that my situation is subject to change.

In Jesus name. Amen.

Song to Ponder: *Trouble don't last always -- Timothy Wright*

--Arleathia Chambliss Wright

Day Sixty

Name a trouble that you have experienced that did not always last. Share a situation that the Lord promised was subject to change?

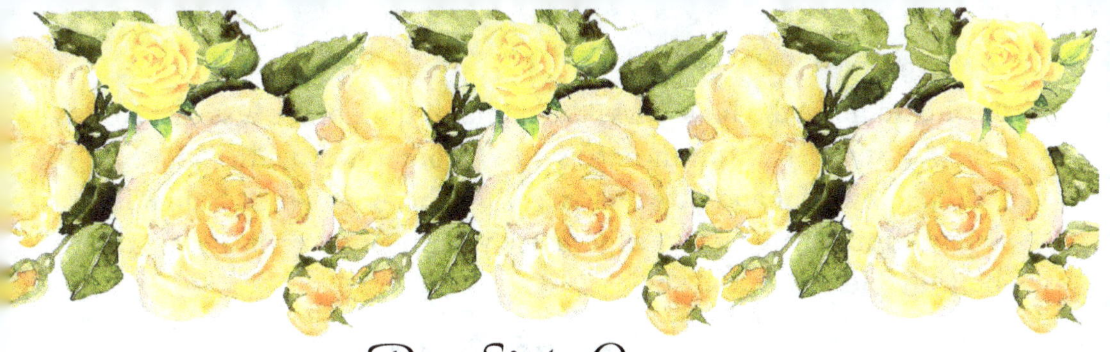

Day Sixty-One

Know God For Yourself

Read: Proverbs 18:10 New King James Version (NKJV)

The name of the Lord is a strong tower;
The righteous run to it and are [a]safe.

God reveals Himself to you only through your experiences with Him. When He reveals Himself to us individually, He describes himself in a new way. That new way describes His awesome character. For example, if you have experienced God during a time of sorrow, He is God the Comforter. When you experience financial difficulties, He is Jehovah Jireh, God the Provider. You know Him as you experience Him.

The names of God describe His awesome characteristics. In the Old Testament, Jehovah is translated "Lord" and Elohim is translated "God." There are many more you may recognize: Jehovah Rapha, our healer, Jehovah Shalom, God of peace, Jehovah Shammah, God who is present, El Shaddai, the almighty God, Elohim, the God above gods, and Jehovah Yahweh, loving, covenant keeping God. God's names will bring comfort during the most troubled times.

There are many names, titles, and descriptions of God in the Bible. They tend to describe people who have a personal experience with Him. He may have been an Advocate for you during a time when your child was treated unfairly. Think of a time, he brought you out the fire without any burns or smoke. The time when He was your Refuge and your Redeemer. Let us use the names of the Lord to uplift Him for who He is and get to know Him for ourselves.

Remember, the bible says "the name of the Lord is a strong fortress, the godly run to him and are safe." In other words, the name of the Lord is powerful and provides safety for those who seek him. So, get to know Him through every experience you encounter with Him. You will be truly blessed.

Let us Pray:

Lord, thank you for revealing yourself to me during the
times I have needed you the most. Thank you that
I can call out to you by name. Thank you for reminding us
that your name reveals your awesome character.
Please help us to embed them in our hearts
and soul preparing us for the times of trouble.
In Jesus name. Amen

Song to Ponder: *I know too much about Him – Smokie Norful*

--Alma Jean Chambliss

Day Sixty-One

Describe ways God has revealed Himself to you through your experiences with Him.

Day Sixty-Two

Flourish Where You Are

Read: Nehemiah 9:21 New King James Version (NKJV)

Forty years You sustained them in the wilderness;
They lacked nothing; Their clothes did not wear out
And their feet did not swell.

I think that in order for me to flourish in some things I would like to do in my life, I have to get out of the mess I am in. Some may say something like "when I get out of jail or trouble; the next time the opportunity comes; after my next project; when I get married; or when I land the promotion; or when I get well. All these examples describe you putting things on hold before you grow stronger, prosper, succeed or do well in life.

Have you ever thought about succeeding and growing stronger during your mess? I mean, would it be amazing to share a testimony telling folks that while you were in the midst of your storm, you wrote a book while in jail; you got promoted before your manager; or you bought a house with bad credit? Must I go on?

In the meantime, follow your dreams and enhance your skills in the midst of your storm.

During the pandemic, you should start planning for your dream job; start your own business; finish college; write the book; pick up a skill; help someone in need. God does not want you to wait until the pandemic is over. He did not say stop pursuing your dreams and believing in Him. Do not wait until the storm is over.

God wants you to flourish where you are, like when He made sure the Israelites did not lack anything. They had all they needed. He will continue to bless and sustain you in the midst of your storm. He also will provide the tools you need to flourish because He knows the plans he has for you.

Let us pray:

Thank you, Lord, that I believe that you will continue to carry me through my mess. Thank you for not leaving me and reminding me to trust in you and not give up the fight. Thanks for reminding me that I can flourish wherever I am in my life.
In Jesus name Amen.

Song to Ponder: *He's concern – CeCe Winans*

--*Arleathia Chambliss Wright*

Day Sixty-Two

Name a time you remained strong in the Lord through your mess?

Day Sixty-Three

Loving One Another

Read: John 13:34-35 New International Version (NIV)

*34 "A new command I give you: Love one another.
As I have loved you, so you must love one another.
35 By this everyone will know that you are
my disciples if you love one another."*

God gave us this new commandment. He wants us to love one another because He first loved us. God demonstrated his love for us when he died on the cross for you and me. He died for our sins to be forgiven and that we have everlasting life. If we do not love each other, then we do not know God. If He is not in your heart, you will despise everything and everybody. He did not say you had to like one another, He said love one another.

Regardless of the circumstances, we must love one another. This is a commandment from God. We may not like the way someone does things, the things someone says, the clothes somebody wears, but we must love them. Where is the love? There is so much hate in this world, love gets lost sometimes. Hate over material things and misunderstandings is brutal. Some of the hate is from the hurt that happened growing up. Some hurts come from parents not showing love. If you misunderstand what love is and cannot express it in the right way, then love is only on the surface of your life. Dig deep within, it's there. God created you with love, that agape love. Love is deep and resides in your heart. We need to stop making excuses that someone did not show us or teach us about love. It is in us. God is within us. Reach within yourself and find what God created with love and break the chains and break the curse.

Oh, what a God we serve. If you put your trust in Him, He will do the rest. That is how much He loves us.

Let us Pray:

Lord, thank you for giving us a new commandment to love one another. Teach us how to show love towards one another. Thank you that you have given us that agape love, that is unconditional. Let us know that love is when we can put our arms around the just and the unjust, the sad and the happy. Thank you for the love that we can feel anyhow, no matter the circumstance. Lord please, shower down your love upon your people. In Jesus name. Amen

Song to Ponder: *Jesus is Love – Smokie Norful & Heather Headley*

--Alma Jean Chambliss

Day Sixty-Three

Describe a time you did not agree with someone or something, but you responded in love because of Jesus command to love one another.

Day Sixty-Four

Trust In God In ALL Things

Matthew 6:32 – 33 New King James Version (NKJV)

32 For after all these things the Gentiles seek. For your heavenly Father knows that you need all these things. 33 But seek first the kingdom of God and His righteousness, and all these things shall be added to you.

Are you mature enough in His word to trust God in ALL things? Are you aware of the blessings that God has bestowed upon you? A songwriter wrote, "Every time I turn around.....Blessings on Blessings." They meant that when you are blessed, you feel invincible. You find yourself thinking that you are unstoppable; that nothing can touch you or get in the way of where you are going with your goals, health, and positive situations. Someone may be having that so-called "easy faith." Faith in knowing and trusting that God provided you with a job, roof over your head, food on the table, and He is covering your family members as they are doing great. Everyone is healthy, bills are paid. Needs are being met continuously. Everything is going well. Because you sought Him first and His righteousness, ALL these things are added to you.

Then, the ultimate happens. Are you mature enough in Him to handle the unexpected? Something out of the ordinary or unusual happens. Something you asked God for has not come to pass when you expected it. You say to God, "Lord, everything was going well. What is happening? My needs were being met, and suddenly, I am having issues with the job, my family members, my finances, limited food on the table, negative thoughts, and my faith has wavered. What changed? I am scared." In Proverbs 3:5-6, the bible said, Trust in the Lord with all your heart and lean not on your own understanding; in all your ways submit to him, and he will make your paths straight. If you are mature in His word and trust in Him, this scripture should come to mind. Meditate on it and be obedient to what it says, and you will be fine.

Let us Pray:

God, thank you for the continuous blessings that you have added to my life. Thank you for being there during unexpected times. I trust you and honor your word that if I seek you first, all these things will be added to me.
In Jesus name Amen.

Song to Ponder: *Blessings on Blessings, Anthony Brown & Group Therapy*

--Arleathia Chambliss Wright

Day Sixty-Four

Name a time you were mature enough in His word to trust God in ALL things? Also, share a time when you were not mature enough in Him to handle the unexpected?

Day Sixty-Five

Protect Your Peace

Read: John 14:27 New King James Version (NKJV)

27 Peace I leave with you, My peace I give to you; not as the world gives do I give to you. Let not your heart be troubled, neither let it be afraid.

Protect your Peace. Jesus left this gift to you. Stay away from the negative energy of your family, friends, and coworkers. When they have drama going on, go the other way. If you have studied the word long enough, you should feel discernment when others are up to no good. The Holy Spirit will let you know if you should be there for someone during their drama. We must be careful that someone else's drama does not dwell in our spirit to bring us down. This disrupts our peace.

The Lord has given us everything we need to live, including Peace. All he asks is that we worship Him. He asks that we do his will. He is the peace that surpasses all understanding. Let's learn to love ourselves and learn to enjoy hanging out with ourselves. I want to be happy, don't you? If I cannot make myself happy, ask God to help me to find happiness and peace within myself. We should not count on someone else to make us happy. Shut out the world around you as best you can. You need peace so you can hear God. You need peace so you can concentrate on the assignment He has for your life that you need to fulfill.

I am happy on the inside and out. No matter the circumstance, I have a smile on my face. I have a good thing going with the Lord, and I am not turning back. If you see me frowning, there's something bad going on. But for the most part, I love people and those who share the same spirit. If love is in our hearts, people with a loving spirit do not want to hurt you. They just want to share the same love towards one another. If I foresee trouble, I will remove myself from the situation as best I can. No hard feelings.

So, welcome in the Lord. Invite him into your heart to help give you that peace you need. We want joy, unspeakable joy. Joy brings peace. Peace comes from the Lord. He is our protector. He will show us life with the pleasures of living with Him.

Let us Pray:

Dear Heavenly Father. I'm so glad I am getting to know you. You left us with the gift of the Holy Spirit which gives peace of mind. I ask that you give me this peace Lord. Give me this peace so that I can hear you and do your will. In Jesus name I pray.

Song to Ponder: *Welcomed In – BeBe & CeCe Winans*

--Alma Jean Chambliss

Day Sixty-Five

Describe ways you protected your gift of peace from outside noise and distractions.

Day Sixty-Six

Grace & Mercy

Read: Psalm 86:15 New International Version (NIV)

But you, O Lord, are a God merciful and gracious, slow to anger and abounding in steadfast love and faithfulness.

Do you really know what Grace & Mercy means? I can tell you what it means to me and how I continue to experience it every day. When God does not punish you for what you deserve, that is His Mercy. And the favor He provides for you, is His Grace.

See, God showed me Mercy when I did not deserve it. He could have punished me, but His grace chose to save me instead. I did not deserve it when people were riding with me while I was drinking and driving and had an accident that could have killed us. Instead, His grace kept us unharmed and alive. I did not deserve it when I disobeyed my mother when she told me not to hang out with the friends who caused trouble. Instead, when trouble came, God's grace showed no fault found against me. I did not deserve His mercy when I lied and stole to keep from getting in a world trouble. Instead, all was forgiven. God showed His mercy to me when I did not trust and obey Him in things that seemed impossible to accomplish and I would do it my own way. Instead, he helped me when I reached a roadblock. Thank you for your grace and mercy, Lord.

God did not punish me when he could have. He continues to show me mercy. I believe He shows me mercy because he knows the plans, he has for me. He knew that I would eventually obey and trust Him fulfilling the purpose He had for me in my near future. I believe with Him showing me mercy also was a lesson for me to learn that my unacceptable actions could have taken a different turn, a turn for the worse. But God.

Mercy is when God does not do to us what we deserve when we do wrong. Grace is what He does for us and the favor He has on our lives. It is the manifestation of His love and compassion for us. So, think about the time He delivered you. When the devil thought he had you. God did not have to do it. When you think about the goodness of the Lord, shout where you are. Remind yourself that He has been good to me, better than I have been to myself. Are you blessed in a way you thought you would never be blessed? It's because of His Grace and Mercy.

Let us Pray:

God, thank you for your grace and mercy that continues to bring me through each and every day. If it had not been for you Lord, the Lord on my side, where would I be. I honor you and bless your holy name.
In Jesus name I pray amen.

Song to Ponder: *Great is your mercy – Donnie McClurkin*

--Arleathia Chambliss Wright

Day Sixty-Six

Mercy is when God does not do to us what we deserve when we do wrong. Grace is what He does for us and the favor He has on our lives. Name a few sins you do not think you deserve favor, grace, and mercy from the Lord.

Day Sixty-Seven

Praying For Others

Read: James 5: 14-16 New King James Version (NKJV)

14 Is anyone among you sick? Let him call for the
elders of the church, and let them pray over him,
anointing him with oil in the name of the Lord.
15 And the prayer of faith will save the sick,
and the Lord will raise him up. And if he has
committed sins, he will be forgiven. 16 [a]
Confess your trespasses to one another, and pray
for one another, that you may be healed.
The effective, [b]fervent prayer of a
righteous man avails much.

God has commanded us to love one another. He also wants us to pray for one another. In order for prayer to work, there must be a prayer of faith. As you pray, you must have faith to believe that what you are praying for will come to pass. The people who offer to pray for you or the people you ask to pray for you must have faith in their prayers for you as well. Not only pray for one another, confess your sins to one another, so you will be healed. For example, if you are sick, and need prayer for healing, once the prayer of faith is initiated, the angels will go to work on your behalf. God will heal you.

The bible talks about the elders. In the church, they would call on the elders to pray in faith over the sick using oils as a simple of God's anointing for healing. The sick were healed by God. The oil represented the physical and spiritual realms of life. It was tangible oil used as medicine for the physical body as the elders spiritually prayed in faith for healing in the name of the Lord.

The scripture tells us the fervent prayers of the righteous avails much. We must confess our sins and pray for one another with passion. We have been equipped to help one another to help them meet their needs. God has put people in our path to help them reach their full potential. They may not be able to reach their destiny without you. Remember, some people come into our lives for a season, reason, or lifetime. We do not know why, but God knows why. There may be an addiction, or challenge that is keeping them from reaching their full potential, and God sent you to help them by praying for them to overcome their fears.

God can do the impossible. Chains of addiction and challenges are broken. It may not happen when we want it, but it is right on time. Sincerely pray for someone and see what happens.

Let Us Pray:

*Father God in Heaven. We come to you today to
pray for our brothers and sisters. Lord, you know what
they stand in the need of. Heal their bodies
and touch their souls today. As the prayers of the righteous
grow stronger every day, help them as they intercede in
prayer to remember that you have all power in your hand.
In Jesus name we pray, Amen.*

Song to Ponder: *Donnie McClurkin & Yolanda Adams - The Prayer*

--Alma Jean Chambliss

Day Sixty-Seven

Describe a time you intercede on behalf of someone else through prayer.

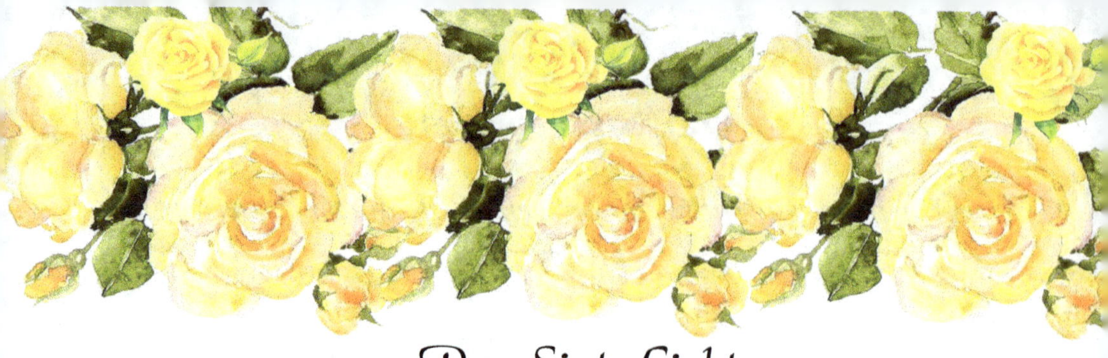

Day Sixty-Eight

Worrying About Tomorrow

Read: Matthew 6:25 – 34 New International Version (NIV)

25 "Therefore I tell you, do not worry about your life, what you will eat or drink; or about your body, what you will wear. Is not life more than food, and the body more than clothes?

Jesus preaches about worry in Matthew 6:25, He says do not worry about life, what you will eat or drink or about your bodies, what you will wear.

We do just the opposite of what is said not to do. We worry about all four, what our life is going to look like, what we will eat, drink and wear. What is so funny, we worry about the food, drinks, and clothes even though we have them in our cabinets, closets, and refrigerators at home. So, imagine the people who do not have as much as you have or any at all. When people do not have these things, He is still saying, they should not worry. He wants us to seek and trust Him. If you have it, be thankful for what you have, and be grateful enough to give to someone who does not have.

Worry contributes to the following: health issues, negative thoughts, mistreatment of others, and reducing your relationship with God. The bible says in verse 34, therefore do not worry about tomorrow, for tomorrow will worry about itself. Each day has enough trouble of its own. Just ask God to help you make it through the day, providing all that is needed with whatever He so desires to provide for you on that day, in Jesus name. When you get to where you are worrying about tomorrow, Rejoice and live for today because yesterday is gone, and there is nothing you can do about it and tomorrow is not promised. Remember, worrying is a sin.

Matthew goes on to say in verse 26 that we should think about the birds in the air. They do not store their food, yet the father provides for them. In other words, don't worry about the needs that God promises to supply. As the saying goes, when you pray, don't worry. When you worry, don't pray.

Seek first his kingdom and his righteousness and these things will be given to you.

Let us Pray:

Father God, I thank you for all that you have provided. Please renew my mind so that I know to seek you first and your righteousness knowing that my needs will be given to me. So, I seek you now to do your will in the name of Jesus, Amen

Song to Ponder: *The Winans – Tomorrow*

--Arleathia Chambliss Wright

Day Sixty-Eight

Name some of the things you worry about and why.

Day Sixty-Nine

How To Help Someone In Need

Read: Luke 6:31 New International Version (NIV)

31 Do to others as you would have them do to you.

In 1965, my husband, Allen Chambliss and I was looking for a larger home and help with our handicapped daughter, Daphany. During my husband's search, he found us a place with an older lady by the name of Sister Roxie Miller. She was an elderly lady in need of someone to help her as well. She also an author of a book titled 'From Salt to Sugar' which sold over 500 copies of which two I have now as a keepsake. She was a great help to us. She would iron and fold our clothes after I washed and brought clothes inside from clothesline. She would also help me dress and feed my daughter. During her stay with us, she talked to us about the Bible and reminded us of what an awesome God we serve. This made me believe more about what the Bible saids in Luke 6:31, "do unto others as you would have them to do unto you." We were there helping each other in need.

Sister Miller lived with us for a while until moving to nursing home where she turned 100 years old. She lived to be 102 years old. I will never forget her. I believe in my heart that God arranged for us to take care of one another. She was a God-fearing woman and truly loved the Lord. I have learned from her that if you trust in God and believe in your heart that we can do all things through Christ who strengthens us.

It is just so nice to be nice. You never know when God why God allow people to come into your life. One thing for sure, He has a plan to fulfill His purpose. So be careful how you treat those around you. You may need them one day.

Let Us Pray:

Father, thank you for allowing Sister Roxie in our life.
She was plenty of help. I know that you orchestrated
this plan for us to help one another in our time of need.
Thank you for teaching us to help one another
and for us to do unto others as you would
have them to do unto you.
In Jesus precious name we pray. Amen

Song to Ponder: *I need you to Survive – Hezekiah Walker*

---Alma Jean Chambliss

Day Sixty-Nine

Describe a time you helped someone in need.

Day Seventy

Much Needed Peace

Read: Mark 4:39 New King James Version (NIV)

39 Then He arose and rebuked the wind, and said to the sea, "Peace,[a] be still!" And the wind ceased and there was a great calm.

I am reminded of the story of disciples on the Sea of Galilee. When the storm started, the wind and waves started rocking their boat. The disciples got scared thinking they were going to drown. They then started looking to find Jesus. Jesus was asleep. Jesus had no worries about the storm. Once they awoke him, Jesus rebuked the wind and spoke to the sea, "Peace, be still." The winds and the waves were obedient and ceased.

Have you ever felt like the storms of life were going to drown you and cried out, "Lord, where are you?" The storms of my life have done everything but drown me, by the Grace of God. There are times you think it is getting better, it gets worse. But God. Not only was the wind blowing and the boat rocking, but the worst could have been a hole in their boat. But God.

The storms of life may include heartbreaks, setbacks, relationships, finances, and sickness. You can overcome these storms by connecting to God. When I could not take it anymore, I called on the Prince of Peace. I told him to say the same three words he spoke for the disciples, "Peace, be still." I needed that kind of peace that only comes from Him. The burden was lifted, and I felt like I could make it. I had to stay connected to Him to survive.

Once you realize that the only way you can make it through your storms with much needed peace, you must stay connected to Him. He will give you that peace.

Let us Pray:

Father, thank you for your peace. The peace that removes the burdens and takes away the tension. Thank you for being the peacemaker. Without you there is no peace. Keep me in perfect peace, in Jesus name I pray, Amen

Song to Ponder: *Kurt Franklin – The Storm is Over now.*

--Arleathia Chambliss Wright

Day Seventy

Name some storms you have encountered and God brought you Peace.

Day Seventy-One

A Spiritual Appetite

Read: 1 Peter 2:1-3 New International Version (NIV)

Therefore, rid yourselves of all malice and all deceit,
hypocrisy, envy, and slander of every kind.
Like newborn babies, crave pure spiritual milk,
so that by it you may grow up in your salvation, now
that you have tasted that the Lord is good.

Do you have a spiritual appetite? How strong is your desire for God's Word? When we become newborn babies in Christ, we yearn the taste for spiritual milk. We need this spiritual milk to grow in His word. It is the very thing that we need to nourish our spirit to increase our growth. The desire for God's holy word is where we find the need for nourishment in Christ. It's a spiritual appetite. As the scripture says, "...taste and see that the Lord is good."

When a newborn baby is fed from a bottle, they hold it tight. As they partake in drinking the milk, they may make noises of enjoyment. They may kick their little legs with happy feet because it tastes so good. As infants in Christ, we should act the same way. Our spiritual appetite should be fulfilled as we hear and receive the Word of God. Cry out to the Lord for the strength of His nourishment to fill our heart, mind, body, soul, and spirit. You can also shout, wave your hands, tap your feet, and clap your hands because you know the Lord is good.

The more He fulfills our spiritual appetite, the more He helps us grow in our salvation. Get rid of these things called malice, envy, deceit, hypocrisy, and slander of every kind. Crave the spiritual milk from the Lord now that you know that He is good.

Let Us Pray:

Father God, help us to get rid of the stuff that is keeping us from salvation. Give us the spiritual milk we need to strengthen us. Help us to fulfill the purpose you have for us through your holy word that creates the nourishment in our hearts, body, and soul. Make us new creatures again. Born to crave your spiritual milk. We ask it all in Jesus name. Amen.

Song to Ponder: *Where the Spirit of the Lord is --- Kirk Franklin*

--Alma Jean Chambliss

Day Seventy-One

Describe a time when you had a spiritual appetite for the Word of God yearning the taste of spiritual milk.

Day Seventy-Two

Sharing God's Truth

Read: 2 Timothy 1:5 New International Version (NIV)

I am reminded of your sincere faith, which first lived in your grandmother Lois and in your mother Eunice and, I am persuaded, now lives in you also.

Second Timothy 1:5 talks about Timothy's heritage from his loved ones like his grandmother and mother. They started the foundation of faith. As Timothy became a spiritual disciple, Paul is reminded of his sincere faith that came from his grandmother, Lois and mother, Eunice. Now that you have grown in your spiritual life, you can become a disciple maker too because of the spiritual foundation your parents and grandparents made for you.

I remember the foundation of faith set out for us as kids growing up attending Sunday school, church services and youth fellowship. Also, my mom and grandmother were having a mission meeting at their homes and my daddy was singing hymns around the house. Growing up, I did not realize that all of this was building a foundation around me for my spiritual life to become a disciple for Christ. I believe it was a plan God has for all of us to grow up as spiritual children and eventually become disciple makers like Jesus.

Matthew 28:19 focuses on the command for multiplying disciples. It states that as disciples, we should go and make disciples, baptizing and teaching others to become disciples as scripture commands it. Imagine if you do not make disciples, the disciples who model God, your effectiveness will have failed God's plan and stops at one generation. Jesus did this with his disciples. He trained them to do what he said to do and how he did them. They later became bold teachers discipling others as Jesus commanded. Paul gives examples and teachings about this.

Creating disciples is necessary because, first, Jesus commands us to do so. If you were born back in the days when Jesus was here, and was one of His disciples trained to model Him, would you pass on His truth? By now, you would be better than ever, and your faith would have strengthened. When people see the changes in you, they would love to have the same spirit that you have.

So, thank God for Jesus. It is not about us. It is about Jesus. Thank Him for giving you the opportunity to model Jesus to fulfill the purpose he has for you. Pray for the obedience to follow his command to pass on his truths to your family and others, in Jesus name.

Let us pray:

Thank you, Father, for all that you have done for me.
Thank you for giving me the opportunity to model Jesus
as best I can to fulfill the purpose you have for my life.
I pray for continuous obedience to follow your command
to pass on Your truths to my family, friends, and enemies.
In Jesus name I pray, Amen.

Song to Ponder: *It's not about us. Bishop Noel Jones*

--Arleathia Chambliss Wright

Day Seventy-Two

Who started the foundation of faith in your life and name some ways it has helped you share with others in your spiritual life?

Day Seventy-Three

Help Your Fellow Brothers And Sisters

Read: 1 John 3:17 New King James Version (NKJV)

17 But whoever has this world's goods, and sees his brother in need, and shuts up his heart from him, how does the love of God abide in him?

If God is in you, why is it so hard to help your brothers and sisters? In 1 John 3:17 it states that if anyone has enough money to live and see a brother or sister in need and not help them, how can God's love be in that person?

I have watch so much of this happen throughout my life. It has happened to me when I have been in need, but because of what others have done to some people, they sometimes mess it up for others who really need that helping hand. Helping can be as simple as providing food, clothing, shelter, or even resources to find out how to get a job, some food, or a place to stay. Some people can be so cruel. But, if they do not have God in them, then you may expect the cruel reaction.

My momma taught me and my siblings how to help one another because that's the way God wanted it. Even though we were helping each other as blood relatives, helping one another became natural with helping other people. It just felt so good. Then I started teaching my children to help each other, and now they love to help their fellow brothers and sisters. It doesn't take much to give, but if you have it to give, do not hesitate to give. When you help someone in need, it activates the power of God, and leaves a good feeling inside.

There was a family who needed help with lodging. A wealthy man who had all that anyone could ask for, would past by this family each day in front of his business. Because of arrogance and pride, he would not consider helping the family. This was so sad. The thing about this man, he would go to church, serve the Lord, and everyone loved his personality, but he would not help a soul. He also claimed to have Christ in him. Do not be like this man.

God wants us to share our abundance with those who are less fortunate. When you bless others, He will surely bless you. The poor and the orphans are examples of people who are homeless and in need from those who have it to give. When we depend on one another for help, we may complement each other's strengths and weaknesses. We are to always help one another. Asking for help is not a sign of weakness, but a mark of unity. If God is in you, let us unite today, and help those in need.

Let Us Pray:

Father God in heaven. Thank you for all that I have.
Help me to be helpful to someone else in need or
less fortunate. For you blessed me, I want to
bless others. In Jesus name.

Song to Ponder: *Be Blessed – Bishop Paul S. Morton*

---*Alma Jean Chambliss*

Day Seventy-Three

Describe a time you have helped your brothers and sisters who were in need.

Day Seventy-Four

Show Love Towards One Another

Read: 1 John 3: 14 & 18 New International Version (NIV)

*14 We know that we have passed from death to
life, because we love each other. Anyone who does not love
remains in death. 18 Dear children, let us not love with
words or speech but with actions and in truth.*

1 John says God wants us to Love one another. The world hates you and everyone who hates his brother are murders and will not have eternal life. We know when we have passed from spiritual death to eternal life when we love our brothers. If you are not convicted when you do wrong to someone, you are not of God. Christlike love for one another is commanded.

Jesus' death on the cross paid the price for our sins and restored the broken relationship we had with God which made it possible to right the relationship with God's children. 1 John says that our love for God reflects our love for one another. So, you may not like someone, because of the things they do or say, but you must love them regardless. Think about it. We continue to love the Lord even when our prayers are not answered right away or when the prayers are not answered the way we thought they should have been. So, whatever your brother or sister says or does, you do not have to like them, but love them always because Jesus commands it.

We are to love others with actions and truth, not just words. Anyone can say I love you. The bible says, "dear children, let us not love with words or tongue but with actions and in truth."

Go and reconcile your relationship with God so that you can live in the word and pray in faith. After you build that vertical relationship, then you will be able to love others as He first loved you through fellowship with believers, witnessing to the world, and ministry to others.

Let us Pray:

Thank you for reminding me to love one another as you love me. I love everyone but may just dislike some of their ways. I know that the punishment is death if I do not love everyone. Loving you reflects my love for others. Thank you for loving me.
In Jesus name I pray. Amen

Song to Ponder: *Jesus is Love – Smokie Norful*

--*Arleathia Chambliss Wright*

Day Seventy-Four

Name a time you have shown love through action and truth.

Day Seventy-Five

Cast Your Cares!

Read: 1 Peter 5:7 New King James Version (NKJV)

Casting all your cares upon him, for he cares for you.

Give all your worries and cares to God. A songwriter has written, take your burdens to the Lord and leave them there. Another songwriter wrote, he is concerned about you. So, when the bible says, cast all your cares to the Lord. Do just that. He did not say some of them, but ALL of them. Listen, God loves you. He carries our heavy loads. He is in control and knows what we can bear. He sees all, knows all and hears all. Release it all to him. Then count it all joy. He cares what happens to us.

God has done so many things for me. When I sent my youngest off to college. I wanted her to succeed more than anything. Knowing what she would have to face in this world, I had to release the burdens of worry and surrender all to the Lord. I had to trust that she would be fine.

When you are born again as a child of God, you trust that he has your back, and he is right there with you. If I believe he would take care of me, then I knew he would take care of her. He did and continues to do so. He cares for all, including our enemies. Oh, what a God we serve.

We are all going through some challenges in our lives. After we suffer for a while, God will restore and strengthen us with all power in his hand. Please stand strong in your faith knowing he cares for you. He is waiting for you, to cast your cares upon Him.

Let Us Pray:

Father, we thank you that all power is in Your hands and not the enemy. Thank you for taking my worries and cares from me. Thank you for sustaining me while I am going through. In Jesus name. Amen

Song to Ponder: *He's concerned about you – CeCe Winans*

--Alma Jean Chambliss

Day Seventy-Five

Describe a time when you cast ALL your burdens on the Lord and left them there for Him.

Day Seventy-Six

Double For Your Trouble

Read: Job 42:10 New King James Version (NKJV)

10 And the Lord [a]restored Job's losses when he prayed for his friends. Indeed, the Lord gave Job twice as much as he had before.

Have you ever experienced a difficult test of your faith that you did not understand? The difficult test may have been struggles with personal or business finances, your children, marriage, illnesses, or loss of loved one. I would add a most difficult test is having not one of these struggles, but more than one at the same time. Then you cry out, "Whew!! Lord, please help me!" There was a time when you were healthy and strong, working things out. Now, you feel helpless, exhausted, and frustrated. These difficult tests can be overwhelming.

Scripture tells us that Job's life was suddenly put to a difficult test of his faith. He lost his family and possessions as well as suffering from a devastating illness. He did not understand the things that was happening to him either, but he stayed the course and things eventually turned around. Job prayed for relief from his distress with repentance. He even prayed for his friends. If you pray for yourself and others, repent, and stay the course during your difficult test, the same will happen with your situation. If you have read the story, Job ended up with twice as much as he had after all. Where you are is not where you will be always. Relief is coming. God will give you double for your trouble if you would remain faithful in Him. Just keep the faith and keep holding on.

Let us Pray:

Thank you for all that you are doing behind the scenes.
During difficult times, Thank you for reminding us that
you are still on the throne, and you are in control.
Thank you for reminding us that this too shall pass.
In Jesus name we pray. Amen

Songs to Ponder: *Keep the Faith – Charles Jenkins*
The best is yet to come. – Tri City Singers & Donald Lawrence

--Arleathia Chambliss Wright

Day Seventy-Six

Name a time where you lost everything or almost everything, and God blessed you with more than enough.

Day Seventy-Seven

Love Your Enemies

Read: Luke 6:27 New International Version (NIV)

27 "But to you who are listening I say: Love your enemies, do good to those who hate you, 28 bless those who curse you, pray for those who mistreat you.

Have you ever been bullied? Or hurt for no reason, mentally, physically, or spiritually? What was your response? These are people we call our enemies. They are people who hurt us. They are the ones who will steal, kill, and destroy the very thing we love. They accuse us of being a threat to them. They hate us and mistreat us. Think about the racism in this world. People who disrespect what others believe in. These people are hurt individuals themselves who take their frustrations out on us. How can you love a person such as this. In the bible Jesus teaches about loving your enemies.

There were Jews who hated the Romans who oppressed God's people, but Jesus told them to love their enemies. He commands us to do so. He wants us to not only love them, but pray for them as well. Be and example. Do not hurt them because they hurt you. Be gentle and kind. You may be protecting them from their own selves. Be merciful as God has been for you.

As a child of God, we want to be obedient to thus says the Lord. It gets hard when you are acting in the flesh. However, we know when to turn it on and off. When we are at work, we are selective of who we curse back. We would probably say a prayer for the mistreatment right away because we do not want to lose our job. When someone says something to us, then we may pray to God, "Lord, keep me from loosing my job today." This situation takes a conscious effort to keep from sinning against the enemy.

Pray for self-control and will power in these types of situations. Remembering what Jesus said is something to keep in mind as well. Being obedient to his word is the key. Situations will turn out much better when we obey the word of God. This also elicits scripture that states to do unto others as you would have them to do unto you. We must love others even if they do not love us. Your reward is greater in heaven.

Let Us Pray:

Father God, thank you for teaching us that love is patient and love is kind. Continue to remind us that there is a great reward for obeying your word. Give us strength, O God, to love our enemies and to do good for those who hate us. We will pray for our enemies as you have commanded.
In Jesus name. Amen

Song to Ponder: *God favored me despite of my enemies—Hezekiah Walker*

--Alma Jean Chambliss

Day Seventy-Seven

Describe a time you were hurt by the enemy and was taught to still love and prayed for them anyways.

Day Seventy-Eight

Start Improving Your Life

Read: Colossians 3:12 New International Version (NIV)

12 Therefore, as God's chosen people, holy and dearly loved, clothe yourselves with compassion, kindness, humility, gentleness and patience.

God has chosen this new life of love for you. Dress in your wardrobe he has picked out for you. We wear some or all these wardrobes every day. We all have a compassion for something we love to do. That compassion may be helping people in need. You may not have much but your heart and compassion allow you to want to help those less fortunate. This is the love God has given you to show compassion to others. Good deeds can go a long way. When you help someone put groceries in their vehicle, carpooling with a coworker, and picking up a neighbor's kid from school when you pick up your kid are all acts of kindness. People are attracted to those who are kind and compassionate. If you show positive attitude towards negative situations, people recognize your potential to be humbling and self-control.

Our attitude has a lot to do with our success in life. If you choose the wardrobes God picked out for you, he will do the rest and anything else is extra.

Let us Pray:

Father God, thank you for improving my life. Thank you for clothing me with compassion, kindness, and humility for other people. It makes me feel good and most of all, I am honoring you. Continue to teach me when times get hard with some people. Bless me as I use the fruit of the Spirit in my attitude. In Jesus name I pray. Amen.

Song to Ponder: *Love --- Kirk Franklin*

----Arleathia Chambliss Wright

Day Seventy-Eight

Describe a time where you were not always willing to demonstrate compassion, kindness, humility, gentleness and patience, but God.

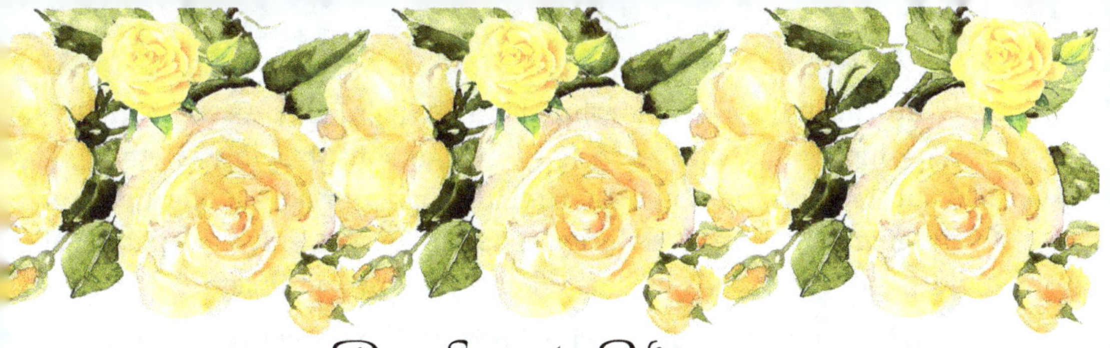

Day Seventy-Nine

When Anxiety Attacks

Read: John 14:27 & Philippians 4:6-7 New King James Version (NKJV)

27 Peace I leave with you, My peace I give to you; not as the world gives do I give to you. Let not your heart be troubled, neither let it be afraid.

6 Be anxious for nothing, but in everything by prayer and supplication, with thanksgiving, let your requests be made known to God; 7 and the peace of God, which surpasses all understanding, will guard your hearts and minds through Christ Jesus.

Haven't you heard the saying, "Don't worry about anything, instead, pray about everything." Why do we worry about anything if we believe in what the gospel tells us? We worry about where our next meal is coming from to who will give us an opportunity of a lifetime. The biggest thing is that we pray, and pray and pray, but when nothing happens better for our situation, we get anxiety and still worry.

God said he will take care of us. He's the provider. He said he would not leave or forsake us. He is our present help in the times of a storm. Tell God thank you for what you do have and what you stand in the need of. He already knows our needs, he just wants you to ask and it shall be given. Seek and he shall find. Knock and the door will be open to you.

There must be a relationship with the almighty God. With this relationship, you should learn not to be anxious, but in everything let all your requests be made to Him through prayer, supplication and thanksgiving. You will experience God's peace which surpasses all understanding which is far marvelous than one can imagine.

As my relationship has grown with Him, I love my peace. A peace of mind goes long way. When you have His peace, you have no anxiety. I know because I have been there. When a storm came through town and caused damage to my house, believe me, I was nervous and worried. This situation caused me to experience anxiety. Instead of trusting God and being obedient to his word and not worrying about anything, I became sick with the anxiety.

Then the Holy Spirit brought two scriptures, John 14:27 and Philippians 4:6-7, to my remembrance. These verses helped me to believe that His word is true and once I begin to believe His word, I begin to have peace and there was no more worrying. I believed that if he has done it before, he will do it again.

Let Us Pray:

Dear Heavenly Father. Thank you for always being there for us when we need you. Thanks for leaving us with the gift of the Holy Spirit which gives of peace of mind. In Jesus name we pray.

Song to Ponder:

--Alma Jean Chambliss

Day Seventy-Nine

Describe a time you were anxious about something, but God gave you peace to endure.

Day Eighty

Take Rest

Read: 2 Corinthians 2:1-2 New International Version (NIV)

So, I made up my mind that I would not make another painful visit to you. 2 For if I grieve you, who is left to make me glad but you whom I have grieved?

People will suck you dry. Are you that person who everyone leans and depends on? They hold you responsible for their needs, wants, and have high expectations for you. You are their hero. These people may be your spouse, kids, other relatives, friends, and even organizations you belong to. They depend on you for everything. Your being so helpful was quite natural with no motive intended to be at their beck and call to where your life is put on hold. Their emergency was not to be your priority all the time. However, you have created a monster. You never say no. They are your Kryptonite. You put off your needs for others. You feel obligated to help. You continue to do so until they have suck you dry. If you decided not to be there for them, they would act like all you did for them never happened. They will then dislike you and mistreat you. This is unhealthy and overwhelming for you. Who will be there for you?

Now, you are tired, and at times, frustrated. You need a break. Do not feel guilty or even selfish for saying no. Cut back the things you are doing and find a balance. You must take care of yourself, or you will be no good for anyone. You need rest to re-energize yourself. Take time for yourself.

Did you know Paul wrote a letter to Corinth letting them know he would not make it to visit them? He was frustrated from his last visit. He was insulted and everything he tried to do for them was challenged. He said no to a commitment, so can you.

Jesus even took a break and went to the mountains to rest and pray. This was with great solitude, quiet place to rest, pray and get away from it all. He had been healing and creating miracles. I am sure that was draining for him. People shouting, "Heal me, touch me, pray for me" and pulling him here and there. People were trying to suck him dry.

Rest as Jesus and Paul did. Protect your tabernacle. You need to rebuild your energy so you can help yourself when others are not around. Allow the Holy Spirit to rest in you.

Let us pray:

Dear Heavenly Father. Thank you for giving me counsel and the spirit of rest. God bless those I cannot attend to right now. Lord, I need you to protect me from overwhelming circumstances of life that includes my family and friends. I trust that you will fill in the gaps that only you can fill. Thanks so much in His precious name. Amen

Song to Ponder: *Take Rest – Deitrick Haddon*

--Arleathia Chambliss Wright

Day Eighty

Describe a time where you you had to take rest in God.

Day Eighty-One

God's Unchanging Hands

Read: Proverbs 3:5-6 New International Version (NIV)

Trust in the Lord with all your heart,
And lean not on your own understanding;
6 In all your ways acknowledge Him,
And He shall [a]direct your paths.

God never changes. He is always the same. Who was there for you every time you were in need? No matter the situation, we know who to reach out to or who we should seek after. Life will throw us twists and turns. We will have ups and downs, but God, he will see us through. I have learned to trust Him in everything. You cannot beat it. He will not fail.

When you think about what the Lord has done for you, that thought should bring you joy. He has done so many things. He has done so many things that it is said, if I had a thousand tongues, I still would not have enough to thank him. God is always the same. Every time you go to him, He releases his power to help you endure your trials and tribulations. When he does these things for us, we must share it with our brothers and sisters. Sharing your testimony will help others understand that God does the same for all of us.

He is the same today, tomorrow, and forevermore. His love is the same. He does not pick and choose who He gives his love to. He is forever faithful and always providing for us.

As the scripture tells us, we must trust in the Lord with all our heart, and not lean onto your own understanding. Trust that He will not leave you. In other words, trust the process. In all your ways, good, bad, and ugly, acknowledge God as your Lord and Savior, and he will direct your paths. The blinders will be removed. You will see things you've never seen before. As the song writer says, build your hopes on things eternal and hold to God's unchanging hand. What he's done for me, he will do it for you. He's given us the same Grace.

Let us Pray:

Thank you, Father, for Your Grace and Your Mercy.
We lift Your Holy name. Thank you for never changing.
Thank you for the same love, kindness, and
protection you give everyone each day. Thanks for being the
same today, tomorrow, and forevermore. We adore
you and worship you. In Jesus name. Amen

Song to Ponder: *Same Grace – William Murphy*

--Alma Jean Chambliss

Day Eighty-One

Describe a time when you did not know how to trust God and lean onto His understanding.

Day Eighty-Two

Drowning In My Transgressions

Read: 2 Samuel 22:17 New International Version

"He reached down from on high and took hold of me; he drew me out of deep waters. Have you felt like you were always drowning in your transgressions?

I can relate to some transgressions I was drowning in that I could not shake. For instance, financial debt. I would put off paying some things just to purchase things that was not necessary or that I wanted immediately. I would put my needs on hold to purchase my wants. I would live above my means as they call it and spending money I did not have. This habit became so powerful that I could not overcome it. It consumed my life. The enemy told me I would be in debt forever, and there was no way out.

If you are facing things that have power over you, there is good news. There is a way out. You may be like me and cannot escape the habit, the bad breaks, or beat that awful disease. But God. The Most-High God is with you through it all. He controls everything, not the enemy. God has a purpose and a plan for all of us. He has the final say. Second Samuel 22:17 tells us that God is going to draw us out of the deep waters and rescue us from those bad things that have power over us. These things are the enemy who tends to hold us back. But God is saying these things are no match to him. He will turn things around.

The enemy is a lie! Jesus paid it all and all to Him I owe. There is a way out. God is Sovereign. He knows all and sees all. He is about to pull you out of your transgressions as He did for me. God has the final say.

Let us Pray:

Dear Heavenly Father, the one who has the final say, thank you for saving me from my transgressions. Although it seemed impossible for me, you made it possible. I realize that you are in control, and I must trust you to bring me through. Thanks for always being with me. Thank you, in Jesus name. Amen.

Song to Ponder: *Deliver Me – Donald Lawrence ft. Le' Andria Johnson*

--Arleathia Chambliss Wright

Day Eighty-Two

Name a time you were drowning in your transgressions and God brought you out.

Day Eighty-Three

Reading And Writing For Comfort

Read: Philippians 4:13 New King James Version (NKJV)

I can do all things through [a]Christ who strengthens me.

I can remember when I was a little girl, my parents bought me a book and crayons all the time to keep me company. Being the only child at the time, they bought them for me to keep me busy. I learned to read and write at the age of 4 and started school when I was 5 years old. I was the smartest child in my class. When I turned 8 years old my mother and I moved to Alex City, Alabama. I was in the second grade, but when we moved there, my mother registered me for the third grade instead. When school was over for the summer, I received my report card and found out I had passed the third grade. I was so happy that I ran all the way home to show my mother. She was so happy and knew that I could do it.

I began to read and write for comfort. I did not have any siblings at the time or many friends so I would just read every book I could find. It was my favorite past time. I started reading the Bible and when I attended Sunday School. Reading the Bible and the stories inside, helped me to believe that I could do anything if I believed in Him and in myself. I learned the scripture that says, I can do all things through [a]Christ who strengthens me. The Lord has truly been a blessing to me. Today, I still read books, but they are more biblical books than coloring books. My relationship with the Lord is stronger than before. Reading His word gives me peace and better understanding of my purpose. I praise Him and I adore Him.

You can do all things if you put your mind to it believing that Christ is the one who strengthens you.

Let Us Pray:

Father God, reading your Word brings me great pleasure.
Pleasure that I have found since I was a little girl.
Thank you for molding and making me who I am today.
It is because of your strength that I enjoy
reading your Word. Continue to minister to me as
I continue to read. Bless those who are reading your word
to share the same experience.
In Jesus name. Amen

Song to Ponder: *Strength – John P. Kee*

--Alma Jean Chambliss

Day Eighty-Three

Describe a time when reading the Bible and writing in a journal became comfort for you.

Day Eighty-Four

Praying Impossible Prayers

Read: James 4: 3 New King James Version (NKJV)

When you ask, you do not receive, because you ask with wrong motives, that you may spend what you get on your pleasures.

Have you ever prayed for the impossible or for something out of the ordinary that you could not happening on your own? I remember a time when the group home reported to my mother that my sister had stopped eating. She had not eaten in a week. My mom kept going back and forth to see if she could get her eat by being there with her. We prayed that she would start eating soon. We would touch and agree asking God to heal whatever was keeping her from eating. I remember the nurses could not figure out why she was not eating after two weeks. Who goes without eating for two weeks? I kept praying, Lord, we do not know what to do. Help the doctors figure this out. Evidently, these were small prayers, not bold prayers.

I am not saying that your prayers must be about the impossible or the size matters. No, no, no. I want you to experience God's mind-blowing miracles from prayers that will change your life. Here is why. I began to take my prayers to the next level. I went to the word and reminded God that I knew exactly who he is. I said, "God, you are strong and mighty; you open doors when we cannot open them; you heal the sick and raise the dead. You created us in our own image; we are your children; you take care of your children. God, I know that the miracle you have created will not die of hunger. I refuse to believe that her life will end like this at 49 years old. You told the doctors, no, when they said she would not live to see 16 years old. Please Jesus. I am begging you. You said we had the same authority as Jesus to touch and heal. I ask you right now in the name of Jesus to give me the anointing power, the same authority to touch and heal my sister, in the name of Jesus." When I arrived there, my sister was in a fetus position and not moving. Her hands and feet were purple and blue which where most of her pain was. I felt the power of Jesus, and I touched her, she screamed a painful sound coming out that position. God immediately told me what to do and I was obedient. I put her in my car and took her to a hospital outside of the area the home care was taking her. The doctors took her in and started working with her immediately. Later, the doctors told me that my actions saved her life. He said she may not have made it to the next day. Glory be to God.

Step outside your comfort zone with confidence in your prayers. If you are praying for your children to stay out of trouble, pray boldly for God to give you double for your trouble. Pray that he not only protects them but give them new direction for their future that seems impossible. James 4:3 says when you ask and do not receive, because you ask amiss, that you may spend what you get on your pleasures. Meaning, you may have asked in the wrong way or with wrong motives. Try another approach by saying 'this too shall pass.' Boldly confess praying a faith filled prayer. Let him know you know where your help comes from. Ask for what you are believing for. Ask for what looks impossible, knowing that He can do the impossible. I thank him for the confidence I had in knowing that he would give me the anointing power to move when I needed to move and go where I needed to go to get help for my sister. Glory be to God.

Let us Pray:

Father God, thank you for hearing my prayers. Thank you for giving me faith and confidence in you. You said in your word, if I remain in you and your words remain in me, ask and it will be given. I praise you and love you in Jesus name. Amen.

Song to Ponder: *I Trust You – James Fortune*

--Arleathia Chambliss Wright

Day Eighty-Four

Name a time you prayed a prayer you thought was impossible for you to accomplish, but it was not impossible for God.

Day Eighty-Five

Love Them Regardless

Read: Luke 6:29-31 New King James Version (NKJV)

27 "But I say to you who hear: Love your enemies,
do good to those who hate you, 28 bless
those who curse you, and pray for those who
spitefully use you. 29 To him who strikes you on
the one cheek, offer the other also.
And from him who takes away your cloak,
do not withhold your tunic either. 30 Give to everyone
who asks of you. And from him who takes away your
goods do not ask them back. 31 And just as you
want men to do to you, you also do to them likewise.

Do you lend money to only the people who you know will pay you back? For those we do not lend money, most of the time, we think about how the person has done us once before or how they have done other people when it comes to money or even favors. Do you think having this type of character is you being a good person? We are supposed to give to anyone who asks, if we have it to give, of course.

Do you love only the people who love you back? We are to love everybody. We tend to love people from a distance making the statement, I love them, but I cannot be around them. Did you know love is more than just a word, it's an action? We can say to someone all day," I love you". Ask yourself, have you shown that person love lately? If not, show some compassion.

We think we are doing good by treating people this way, but this is not pleasing in God's eyes. We are so focused on the person not repaying us or how others love us, that we have no compassion as God our father has for us. You must love one another, including your enemies. He said to love your enemies, do good to those who hate you and bless and pray for them. Do good to the ones who persecute you regardless of how they treat you. It's the right thing to do.

Let Us Pray:

Father God, help us to love others regardless to what they have done to us. For You said it in Your word to love our enemies and do good to those who hate us. Deliver us, Jesus. Help us to learn to pray for those who use us. Give us the understanding and the know-how to obey this command which pleases You. In Jesus name we pray, Amen

Song to Ponder: *Deliver Me – LeAndria Johnson*

--Alma Jean Chambliss

Day Eighty-Five

Describe a time you found it hard to forgive your enemy.

Day Eighty-Six

Your Prayer Privilege

Read: John 15:7 New International Version (NIV)

7 If you remain in me and my words remain in you, ask whatever you wish, and it will be done for you.

When we pray, angels go to work on our behalf. When we pray, we are having a conversation with the Spirit of God. Having a conversation with Him can seem hard for us at times. If we continue to study his word, we will learn that there is a certain approach, attitude, and posture we must have when praying to God. The approach must be with a humbling attitude, acknowledging him with great honor and stature. Our posture must be filled with confidence that he is Lord and knowing that he hears our prayer. When we go to the throne of our Father, there must be no doubt that we are his children. If we can do this, there is no right or wrong way to pray.

Prayer privilege is because of Jesus. We cannot go to the Father except through Jesus Christ. We cannot make our requests known to God without it being in Jesus name. So, at the end of every prayer, remember to say, all this "in Jesus name", Amen. I guarantee his supernatural power will occur, providing all that you ask for and more. Once you make Jesus first in your life, you can start building a relationship with God. To build that relationship, it starts by living in His Word, reading, and meditating on it day and night. Then, pray in faith. If Jesus is at the center of your life, and His word is in you, then you can pray and ask for whatever you wish. Jesus said in John 15:7, if you remain in me and my words remain in you, ask whatever you wish, and it will be done for you. which gives insight into how powerful this connection with God through Scripture and prayer can be. This is a great way to communicate with GOD and HE communicates with you.

Let us Pray:

Dear Father in Heaven. We come to you as humbling as we know how thanking you and honoring you for who you are and all you have done. We bless you for hearing our prayers and responding when you see fit. Thank you for the supernatural encounters you have given us that surpasses my understanding. We are so thankful for the path that Jesus has made for us giving us the privilege to speak to you whenever we choose to. In your son's loving name, we pray. Amen.

Song to Ponder: *What a friend we have in Jesus – Spiritual Hymn*

--Arleathia Chambliss Wright

Day Eighty-Six

Describe a conversation you have had with the Spirit of God. What was your approach?

Day Eighty-Seven

The Right Path

Psalm 25:1&4 New International Version (NIV)

In you, Lord my God, I put my trust.
Show me your ways, Lord, teach me your paths.

Have you ever been on a path that you were sure God was taking you and begin to question the delays, distractions, and diversions? There are times we are confused about our path and need some answers from the Lord. You begin to experience disbelief. You saw what looked like you were on the right path, then you felt a 'curve ball', darkness, and the opposite of your belief. I experienced this as a little girl, while being married, and having my children.

As a little girl, I wanted to leave home, get married and have children of my own who would love me. I tried to do everything right. I helped raise my momma's children and my daddy's children. After raising them, I was ready for my own children. My prayer was for God to show me how to stay on the right path and order my steps pointing me in the right direction. It took so long and there were so many distractions and delays. But I trusted Him.

God's plan was bigger than I imagined. I had no idea about this journey I live. As I trusted Him, my future husband came along. Once we were married, he and I had five wonderful children who loved us dearly. I asked God to show us His ways on raising our children. I trusted

Him. We were very happy and still blessed and highly favored today.

First, remember who God is. He is the one who knows all, sees all, and hears all. He is not a God of confusion. He is in control of everything. Trust the process. Just because it seems to be taking a long time, does not mean you are on the wrong path. God has a plan to get you on the right path. In Jeremiah 29:11 the Lord says, "For I know the plans I have for you," plans to prosper you and not to harm you, plans to give you hope and a future". So, continue to keep praying this simple prayer from Psalm 25:1&4. Doors will open and those things you believed in will come to pass. God is up to something. Be encouraged even when you do not see any positive changes. Trust the process; trust God.

Let us Pray:

O Father, how great thou art. Thank you for
working behind the scenes creating a plan bigger than I
had imagined. "In You, I put my trust.
Show me your ways and teach me your paths."
Thank you for ordering my steps even when
I was discouraged. Thank you for giving me a family of
my own who have been more loving than anything
I could ever ask for. Thanks for leading me on the right
path, that was most rewarding.
In Jesus name. Amen

Song to Ponder: *I will trust in the Lord. – Baptist Hymn*

--Alma Jean Chambliss

Day Eighty-Seven

Describe a time when you were on a path that you were sure God was taking you and begin to question the delays, distractions, and diversions.

Day Eighty-Eight

Blessings

Read: Deuteronomy 28:2 New King James Version (NKJV)

And all these blessings shall come upon you and overtake you, because you obey the voice of the LORD your God.

God has provided more for me in my life than I would not have ever imagined. The odds of being a young lady pregnant in college, being a single mom for 27 years, job changes, broken relationships, and financial debts were against me. But God was there for me. He has blessed me with things that I never asked for or dreamed of. All the things I asked for that I can remember seemed reasonable to me like praying for my child, my family, a good job, roof over head, and a good man. It is as simple as that.

We must have a new way of thinking. God has bigger things in store for us which is something out of the ordinary and something unimaginable. So unexplainable that it would blow your mind. What I have learned, when you start building a relationship with God, doing your best to doing His will, the unthinkable happens. That new job, new love, and new beginnings will come to you. Blessings will track you down, good people will want to be in your circle, chains are broken, and mistakes are covered up.

Blessings will sideswipe you like you sitting in your car and overwhelm you. When you keep God first and abide in Him, you better be ready for blessings on blessings, in Jesus name.

Let us Pray:

Father God, thank you for your unexplainable and unconditional love. Your love is free, free indeed. Thanks for providing a way out of no way, blessings on blessings. You said because of my obedience, all these blessings shall come upon me and overtake me. Thank you for all the blessings I've received thus far in
Jesus name I pray. Amen

Song to Ponder: *Your Love – William Murphy*

--Arleathia Chambliss Wright

Day Eighty-Eight

Describe a time He blessed you with things that you would have never asked for or dreamed of.

Day Eighty-Nine

He's Greater than Anything

Read: 1 John 4:4 New International Version (NIV)

You, dear children, are from God and have overcome them, because the one who is in you is greater than the one who is in the world.

I have allowed Satan's voice to overtake my thoughts at times. He convinces me to talk myself out of many things saying what I can and cannot do. I took on the fear of the unknown. I felt defeated a lot of times when things were not going in the right direction. I often thought I could do things on my own to correct the situation. I negated the fact that I could always call on the Lord. The world is so loud and full of distractions that overpowered my thoughts. The devil is out to kill, steal, and destroy you. He is in your ear right now saying 'you can't', and 'you're weak'. He thinks he has the upper hand on things like your relationships, arguments, your children failing in school, and your debt, debt collectors calling.

I have good news. Our God is bigger, stronger, and a healer. God is still on the throne. You are His children. He speaks louder than any enemy. He is speaking to you letting you know that all things are possible through Him. If it is His will, yes, you can, and you are strong. He has his hands of protection over you when he open doors for you. He said to fear no man, but him. If you would just look to the hills which cometh your help, your help comes from the Lord. God is already there. He has overcome these obstacles for you. Just trust and believe in him. He's got you. He is the almighty God, greater than anything. Search within yourself. He is in you. As 1 John 4:4 says, greater is He who is in me than the one who is in the world. Believe it and receive it, in the Name of Jesus. God stands for us.

Let us Pray:

Father God, thank you for being a part of me. Thank you for reminding me that You are greater than my enemy and that I should call upon your name in my times of need. You are Almighty, magnificent, and greater than anything.
In Jesus name. Amen.

Song to Ponder: *Our God – Micah Stampley*

--Arleathia Chambliss Wright

Day Eighty-Nine

Describe a time God was greater than your adversity.

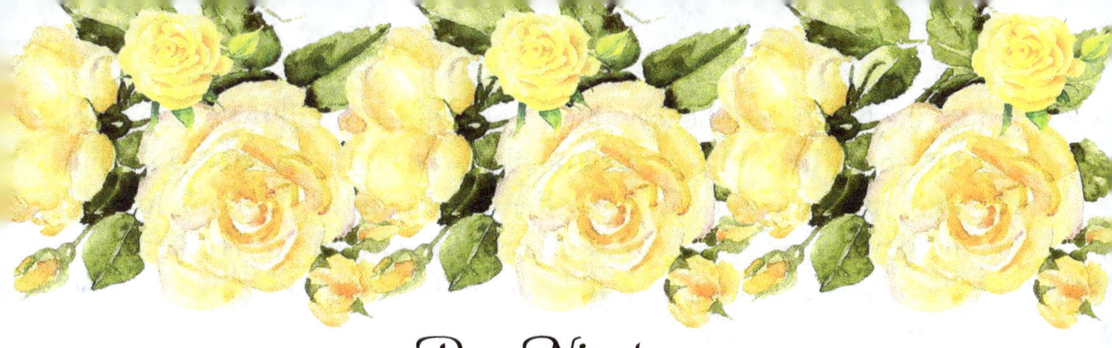

Day Ninety

Ignore The Lion

Read: 1 Peter 5:8 New International Version (NIV)

Be alert and of sober mind. Your enemy the devil prowls around like a roaring lion looking for someone to devour.

Has anyone told you what you could or could not do? Or have you told yourself that you could or could not do it? I think most of us have been told this in some shape, form, or fashion.

I personally have been told I would not make it with a six-grade education; I received my Associates degree in Business in my fifties. I was told we would have to live in the project housing; we built a house I've been in for over 40 years. We were told our daughter who had cerebral palsy would not live past sixteen; she lived to almost fifty. I did not believe I had true friends; the Almighty God, my siblings, my children, and the rest of my family were my closest friends.

As I continued to study to understand God's promise for me, I kept believing in my heart that these things would come to pass one day. The enemy often comes to steal, kill, and destroy your thoughts like a roaring Lion. Of course, there were doubts, but I kept believing all things are possible in Him who loves me. The lion's purpose is to intimidate, and cause fear and anxiety to get his opponent to back down or to give up.

We are fighting those thoughts that roar in every area of our lives. Thoughts that you can't, that you are not good enough, or you will not survive is the roaring lion coming after you. Do not believe the roars.

Ignore the lion. If you believe them, you will not fulfill the destiny God has for you. The things I mentioned I was told I couldn't do. Faith, relationship, and endurance were the key. I ignored the lion's roar. He had no power over my circumstances. I did not bend or break. I thank God because he was in the middle of it all. Lions have a big roar but like giants, they do fall.

As the songwriter says, "don't let anybody tell you that you are not great or that you're not fearfully and wonderfully made. You're special, designer's original. It doesn't matter what they say or do. All that matters is how you feel about you."

Let Us Pray:

Father God thank you for reminding us that we are enough. That you gave us enough. We are made in the image of you. You are in control. You're always there. You are the one who orders our steps. You are the one who said so. In Jesus name, Amen

Song to Ponder: *Enough - Anthony Brown*

--Alma Jean Chambliss

Day Ninety

Describe a time when someone told you what you could or could not accomplish..

Acknowledgements

To My Dearest Johnny Wright,

With the completion of this book, I am overwhelmed with gratitude for the unwavering support you have provided throughout this journey. Writing my first book has been a dream come true, and your love and encouragement have been the cornerstone of my success.

You stood by me during the late nights and early mornings, offering a listening ear when my thoughts were overflowing and when they hit a brick wall. Your belief in my abilities never wavered, even when my own confidence did.

Your patience knew no bounds, whether it was giving me space to write or showing me love when I needed it most. Your unwavering faith in me propelled me forward when doubts crept in.

But beyond the tangible support, it's your love that has truly fueled this journey. Your sense of humor and your presence have been my motivation. You've celebrated my successes and provided solace during moments of despair.

This book is a reflection of not just my dreams, but our dreams, our shared triumphs, and the beautiful partnership we've built together. As I pen down these words, I can't help but think of how blessed I am to have you as my husband, my confidant, and my best friend.

Thank you for being my rock, my inspiration, and my biggest supporter. I love you more than words can express, and I'm eternally grateful for your love and encouragement.

To Our Beloved Family and Friends,
Dianne Boone & Gerald Clark,

As we stand on the threshold of sharing our first book with the world, we are filled with profound gratitude for the unwavering support and invaluable assistance we have received from each of you. Writing a book is a labor of love, but it is your love and commitment to our dream that have truly illuminated this path. Your willingness to lend your time and expertise as proofreaders has been instrumental in shaping this manuscript into its best form. Each page, each sentence, and every word bear the imprint of your meticulous eyes and discerning minds. Your keen attention to detail, thoughtful suggestions, and dedication to the task at hand have helped us refine our work to the highest standard.

Our book is a testament to the power of collaboration and the strength of the bonds we share as family and friends. It is your fingerprints that grace these pages, and your hearts that breathe life into the narrative. With deep appreciation, we acknowledge your role in bringing this dream to fruition. The launch of this book is as much your accomplishment as it is ours, and we will forever be grateful for your contribution to this journey. As we release these words into the world, we carry your love and support with us, knowing that we are surrounded by a circle of loved ones who have made this achievement possible. From the bottom of our hearts, thank you for being part of this remarkable chapter in our lives.

My Dear Friend and Business Partner, Christina Sanders,

As I sit down to pen this acknowledgment, I find it difficult to put into words the depth of our gratitude. Your unwavering support and the boundless creativity you've infused into the journey of launching my first book with my mom are beyond measure.

From the very beginning, you saw potential where others might have seen only challenges. Your gifts and creative ideas have been the catalysts that transformed our vision into reality. Your keen insights and tireless dedication have breathed life into every page, cover design, and marketing strategy. Your contributions have been nothing short of remarkable. But it's not just your skills that have made this journey memorable; it's your heart. Your genuine passion for our project, your endless enthusiasm, and your willingness to go the extra mile have touched us deeply. Your belief in our story and your dedication to sharing it with the world have been nothing short of inspiring.

You've been our guiding star, leading us through the maze of publishing, marketing, and all the intricate details we never could have navigated without you. Your guidance has been invaluable, and your friendship even more so.

This book launch is a testament to what can be achieved when talent, creativity, and friendship come together. It wouldn't have been possible without you, and for that, we are forever indebted to you. In the pages of this book, your spirit lives on, and your name will forever be etched in our hearts as the driving force behind its success. My mom and I are blessed to have you in our lives, not just as a business partner, but as a dear friend and sister.

Thank you, from the bottom of our hearts, for helping us bring our dream to fruition. Your kindness and generosity will never be forgotten.

Blissful Devotions Spotify Playlist

Scan the QR Code to Listen on Spotify

Enjoy a collection of devotional music that will inspire and uplift you. This playlist features a variety of artists and genres, so there's something for everyone.

www.achambliss.com

www.ingramcontent.com/pod-product-compliance
Lightning Source LLC
Chambersburg PA
CBHW050324010526
44119CB00003B/92
* 9 7 9 8 9 8 7 5 3 5 8 0 6 *